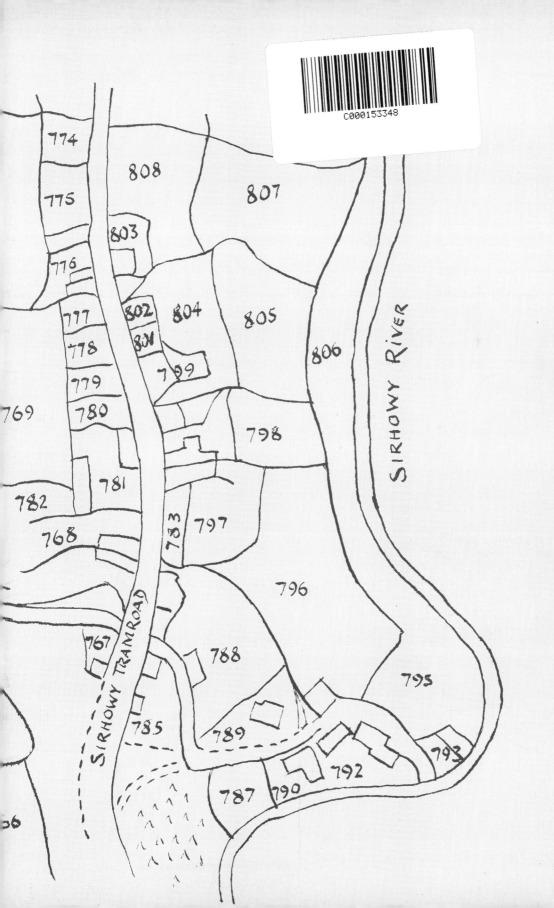

To Hera

Mid-Valley Nostalgia

BLACKWOOD — ARGOED
MARKHAM — HOLLYBUSH

My Love & Good Wishes

William

December 1990

COPIES CAN BE OBTAINED FROM THE AUTHOR
at 31 Church Road, Caldicot, Gwent NP6 4HN

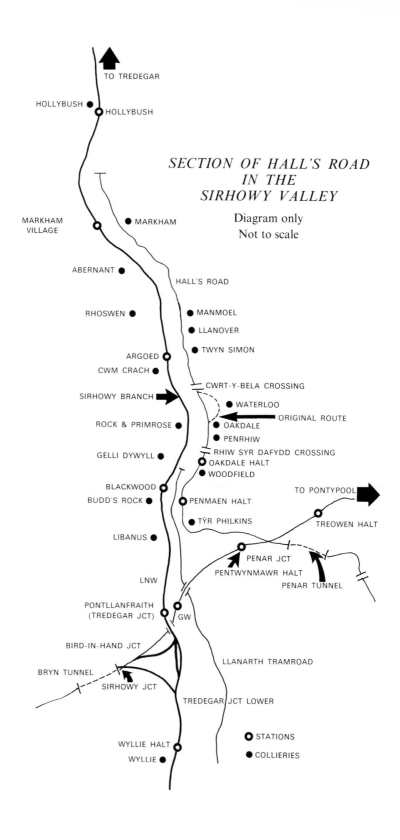

SECTION OF HALL'S ROAD
IN THE
SIRHOWY VALLEY

Diagram only
Not to scale

Mid-Valley Nostalgia

BLACKWOOD — ARGOED
MARKHAM — HOLLYBUSH

W. W. Tasker

1990

D. BROWN & SONS LIMITED

COWBRIDGE

First published 1990

© W. W. Tasker, 1990

ISBN 1 872808 07 7

Title page illustration:
Argoed Mill, Cwm Corrwg.
Drawn from an old faded sepia print on loan from
the late Edward Williams, Argoed (Melin yr Argoed Ucha)

DESIGNED AND PRINTED IN WALES BY
D. Brown and Sons Ltd., Cowbridge and Bridgend, South Wales

Contents

Acknowledgements

I wish to acknowledge with thanks the help given to me by the following—

Newport Museum & Art Gallery.
Newport Reference Library.
Industrial & Maritime Museum (Library), Cardiff.
National Library of Wales, Aberystwyth.
University of Cardiff (Music Dept).
Presenting Monmouthshire (various copies)
Extracts from—

The South Wales Argus, Maesglas, Newport.
The Monmouthshire Merlin.
History of British Buses—South Wales.
David Holding & Tony Moyes—Ian Allan Ltd.

I am also most grateful to those listed below who have provided valuable information and photographs.

Mr. Gerald Davies, Mr. Wayne Hopkins, Mr. W. R. Hamer, Mr. & Mrs. Malcolm James, Mr. Cyril Davies, Mr. Bill Williams, Mr. George James, Mr. Cyril Jones, Mr. & Mrs. Wilson, Mr. Colin Spencer, Mrs. Olwen Hemming, Mrs. C. Prosser, Miss Dolly Lewis, Mr. & Mrs. Esau, Rev. R. J. Young BA, Rev. David Howarth BA, Mrs. Janet Morris (Headmistress, Libanus School', Mr. Geoff Williams, Mr. David Mills, Mr. T. P. Jones, Miss Moyanne Monday, Miss L. Bowditch BA, Mrs. Lucinda Haque, Mr. Adrain Burton (Senior Group Librarian, Pontypridd), Mr. L. J. Harris (General Secretary, Permanent Way Institution), Mr. Brian Mills, Mr. & Mrs. G. Blackford, Mr. J. H. Jenkins, Mr. T. N. Charles, Mr. J. Lewis and Mr. Gurnos Harris.

Introduction

Towards the end of the 19th century families were drawn to the mining valleys of South Wales from Somerset, Gloucestershire and the Forest of Dean; quite a few mastered the Welsh language, many becoming members of the various chapels and Temperance Movements in the district, whilst others liked their pint; hence the boom in the Beer House trade. Many houses were erected by local contractors. Most of the collieries consisted of Headings or Levels; the pits came later.

We begin our journey on the Mynyddislwyn side of the Sirhowy River in the vicinity of Tŷr Philkins and Woodfield, then up through the Rhiw to Gwrhay and Cwrt-y-bela, taking the Cwm road to Cwm Corrwg, and continuing up the steep hill to the village of Argoed, not forgetting Cwm Crach Colliery—more collieries to follow—Llanover and Abernant, then up the Zig-Zag to Manmoel, and a quick return to Bedwellty, coming out into the village and mountain road north of the church, and on to the villages of Markham and Hollybush. To complete our escapade we take the New Road (completed in 1894!) to our journey's end at Blackwood.

I can remember this road when it was more like a country lane in places and very narrow. Gas lamps were to be seen at junctions and crossroads, and in the villages, and lighters were employed to operate them. There was a hill at the Rock near Primrose Colliery (always referred to as The Rock Hill) and a part of it is still there up on the right bank as you look down the valley. The Smith's and Wheelwright's shops on the roadside was where I remember cartwheels being made and iron bands shrunk on hot, and the Smith made our Hoops and Guiders from ⅜″ iron rod. Blacksmiths at the Rock date back to the 18th century—names like John Hopkins, James Lewis, John Dalby, and William Morgan, in 1908. Shoeing a horse in 1850 cost 1/4d!

I trust readers will enjoy this nostalgic picture of this part of the Sirhowy Valley and its people, customs, and way of life.

By the same author—

Railways in the Sirhowy Valley. 1978. The Oakwood Press.
(About to be revised)

The Merthyr, Tredegar & Abergavenny Railway & Branches. 1986.
Oxford Publishing Company.

"I spent many a happy day
On Sirhowy's banks so gay
Gathering nuts that grew about
And deceiving the old trout!"

Green pastures, woodland, whitewashed cottages and hill farms; and the corn mill at Cwm Corrwg, turned by the Sirhowy River—that was the picture prior to the working of the coal measures in the Sirhowy Valley.

Archdeacon Coxe in his book 'An Historical Tour in Monmouthshire' published in two volumes in 1801, had this to say:—

'The features of the Vale are more wild and romantic than those of the Ebwy; it is narrower and deeper''.

Writing of his walk from Bedwellty down to the river he says—'A lane winds from Bedwellty down to the steep sides of a rugged declivity to the banks of the Sorwy; where a bold stone bridge of a single arch is thrown over the rocky channel—the view from the bridge is peculiarly wild, the glen diminished to a hollow between steep and lofty eminences covered with forests. In this solitary spot, a peasant has fixed his cottage and cleared a small piece of pasture ground on the edge of the river'.

(This must surely be the cottage (now demolished) by Pont Syr Dafydd, near the Rock).

Another extract from Coxe's book reads as follows:—

'The beautiful valleys of the Ebwy and Sorwy appear in the hollows between the mountains, deeply shaded with trees and watered by torrents which faintly glimmer through the intervening foliage'.

There was little to do in those days except fish and gather nuts; the only employment then was the occasional work on the hill farms, with very little money and many worked for their keep only. The working of the minerals changed all that when the Argoed and Blackwood district was invaded by prospectors, who bought or leased ground, with mineral rights from the local landowners. It was like Bonanza Creek and the Klondike Goldrush in North-West Canada—the only difference was the colour, the Black Diamond!

Thomas Price bought leases of land, with a right to work in Bedwellty from 1756, and Rosser Thomas and Moses Moses had a lease in 1811 to work coal under Cae Minion, Bedwellty. In 1812, Moses Moses, William Gold and Thomas Webb, trading as the Argoed & Newport Coal Company were working coal under Argoed Ganol and Argoed Fach. In 1817 a lease was granted to the Gelli Dwill Coal Company to work coal under Gelli Dwill Farm. (The spelling is shown as 'Gelli Dywyll' on the O.S. Map). A Mr. Smithers had collieries at Gwrhay and Waterloo, and estimated before a Government Commission that his dues on Bedwellty and other collieries were between £3,000 and £4,000 per annum. Smithers leased mineral land from Sir Henry Protheroe at Cwrt-y-bela, Gwrhay and Waterloo extending in all, to nearly 3,000 acres. Benjamin Hall also advanced Moses Moses £800 towards the erection of a weighing machine, houses and workshops at the Waterloo Colliery which was situated at the bottom of Penrhiwbenji Hill near the Gwrhay. Sir Henry Protheroe and Sir Robert Salisbury also owned collieries in the district, as did Roger Lewis of the Gwrhay, Sir Thomas Phillips, and E. D. Williams, who are dealt with elsewhere in the book. There was much trespassing of underground boundaries between these various companies.

Wages paid top Colliers in the 1780-1820 period was 1/4d per day; Assistants, 1/2d and Girls, for unloading, 6d.

Pollution from the Ironworks and Collieries, coupled later with raw sewage soon destroyed life in the Sirhowy River. Slag heaps began to appear, and the general appearance of the Valley worsened, although when compared with the adjoining valleys, the Sirhowy had a much cleaner look about it, and maintained this over the years. Fortunately for conservationists, the valley is slowly reverting back to the scene described by Archdeacon Coxe in 1800, but it is also having severe side-effects on industry and consequent unemployment.

The Sirhowy Tramroad

The main development, in the beginning of the 19th century was, of course, the building of the Sirhowy Tramroad, and there was no housing of any consequence in the valley before this. The exception perhaps, was the Corn Mill and Flannel Factory, including a few cottages at Cwm Corrwg, Argoed and at nearby Gwrhay. It was completed about 1805, and a Turnpike road ran parallel with it from Tredegar down the Valley.

The villages of Argoed and Blackwood came after, and were built on each side of the Tramroad, with no fence between them. The place names indicate the scene—Hollybush (Llwyn Celwyn) no doubt, because of the presence of Holly Trees in the area. Argoed (Ar-Goed) on the wood, and Blackwood (Coed-Deon), although John Hodder Moggridge tried to change Blackwood into Tremoggeridge! Moggridge lived at Woodfield House, Blackwood, and owned land in the area; he was also a social reformer, giving tenants ground to grow their own crops.

The Valley's Name

In the 18th century, the river from which the valley takes its name of 'Sirhowy' was shown as 'Sorrwy' by Anglo-Norman historians. The 'Gwentian' or 'Glewysian' natives of the 15th-18th century called the river, and spelled it 'Corrwy'. It afterwards became 'Sorwy', then 'Sirhowey', and finally the modern 'Sirhowy'.

Sirhowy - (Sor-way) :— Sor - Angry. Wy-Water.

Bridges over the river in our area are at Pont-Abernant-y-felin, Pont Cwm-Corrwg, Pont Syr Dafydd, and at Pont Ynys-pwll-du. (Rock & Fountain).

The Twin-Kings of the Earth

The Twin-Kings of the Earth—Iron and Coal, were to form the mainstay in the Sirhowy Valley from roughly 1800. Coal is mentioned by several ancient writers—Theophrastus, Siculus, St. Augustine, and many others, and it was probably known to the Roman occupants of this Island. Cinders and pieces of coal having been found in Roman roads and walls, and Roman coins in beds of cinders. There is also historical evidence of coal having been known in the 9th century during the Saxon occupation. It is also mentioned shortly after the Norman Conquest.

It may well be that the Monks were the first miners in South Wales—it is recorded that the Monks of Neath Abbey were getting coal for Iron making in the 13th century, and it seems that the Monks from Glastonbury Abbey were using coal when they visited the old monastery or Church building at Manmoel. This building is now known as Tyr Capel Farm, where chickens drank from an old church font. Mrs. George Phillips gave, some years ago, an interesting account of the farm's association with Glastonbury Abbey which dates back to 1122. In her garden grew the old fashioned Mullein, which was also to be seen growing at Glastonbury Abbey.

After flowering, the monks soaked the stems in mutton fat and used them for lighting purposes.

The Steam Engine

Traffic on the Tramroad was horse-drawn until 1829, but just before Christmas of that year there was great excitement, as the first steam locomotive named 'Britannia' passed down through Argoed and Black-wood on its way to Sir Charles Morgan's Cattle Show at Cwrt-y-bela Farm, Newport. The Sirhowy Tramroad Company was making history, as all this happened in the same year as the appearance of Stephenson's 'Rocket' and the Rainhill Trials of 1829.

About nine locomotives were built at Tredegar between 1832 and 1853 and the villages of Argoed and Blackwood saw names on the engines they would never see again in the railway's history—names like 'ST. DAVID',

11

'TREDEGAR', 'JANE', 'FANNY', 'LORD RODNEY', 'LADY SALE', 'PRINCE ALBERT', 'CHARLOTTE'—and the last built, 'BEDWELL- TY'in 1853. As the number of steam locomotives increased horses became less numerous and by 1860, when the Tramroad was converted into the Sirhowy Railway, they had disappeared altogether. In the conversion, the new line was diverted to the back of the main street in Argoed and Blackwood, and built up on an embankment; as we knew it before closure in 1960.

A limited horse-drawn passenger service on the tramroad was introduced by John Kingston of Newport in 1822. It was known locally as the 'Cara-van'. 'Slater's 1850 Directory' mentions a service from Newport to Trede-gar by Henry Morgan on the Tramroad. There was also a 'Waterloo' Coach run by George Stokes and John Williams on Wednesdays and Saturdays from the Rose & Thistle, Newport. Mail for the Sirhowy Valley went from the Tredegar Arms, Newport every morning at 8.30 a.m.

The Sirhowy Railway passenger service between Sirhowy and Newport commenced on 19th June, 1865. Celebrations of the occasion were aban-doned because of the recent disaster at the Bedwellty Pits Colliery, where 26 men were killed and many injured.

A Report of the opening by the 'Monmouthshire Merlin' is extracted below:—

OPENING OF SIRHOWY RAILWAY

'Last Monday the Sirhowy Railway was opened for passenger traffic, and the important advantages thereby conferred on the public of the district traversed by the line, may be gathered from the anxiety with which for months the event has been anticipated. The inauguration of this improved means of transit was to have been celebrated by great rejoicings; but in consequence of the calamity at the Bedwellty pit on the previous Friday all idea of a demonstration was of course aban-doned. The object of the Sirhowy Railway is to bring Tredegar and Sirhowy, and adjacent collieries and works, into closer communica-tion with the port of Newport. It is between fourteen and fifteen miles in length, and, starting from Sirhowy—which is practically one with Tredegar, the two forming the centre of a considerable population, principally employed at the important and growing works there con-ducted—runs through a beautifully wooded and picturesque valley down to Nine-mile Point, where a junction is effected with the Mon-mouthshire Railway Company's line, over which the Sirhowy have running powers to Newport, and into the Dock Street station. But the route of the Sirhowy has other recommendations than those to be found in its romantic natural scenery: it is opulent in rich mineral seams, and these can hardly fail of being largely developed by the improved railway communication now completed, and in the absence of which many parts of the district now easily reached, have long been most difficult of access. At Tredegar Junction, in the neighbourhood of Blackwood, a junction is formed with the West Midland loop line which unites Merthyr and the West Midlands system at the Pontypool road; and it is intended to extend the Sirhowy line to Nantybwch, where it will join the Merthyr, Tredegar, and Abergavenny Railway, which is leased to the London and North Western Company. Mr. S. Yockney is the general manager, and Mr. R. Bond is the traffic manager, and in these gentlemen the company will, we doubt not, find able and trustworthy officials. It is hoped the Sirhowy line will in its future realise all the glowing predictions which have been from time to time indulged in concerning it. It will be observed that Mr. T. B. Batchelor, at the half yearly meeting of the Monmouthshire Company (reported on another page), again drew attention to the importance of the Sirhowy being acquired by that company'.

A very informative guide for the area was the Rev. Emilus Nicholson's 'Cambrian Guide', published in 1840:—

'Coming from Pontypool, through Crumlin, the road proceeds up the hill leading to Croespenmaen, the Argoed, Bedwellty and leading to Tredegar, but on account of its uneveness is not frequently used except to Penmaen. Turning to the right there is a good carriage road, which runs parallel all the way. This is the best road from Pontypool to Tredegar and Merthyr Tydfil. Nearly opposite on the hill to the left is Penllwyn, a large old Mansion, surrounded by high sycamore trees, now occupied as a farmhouse. One and a half miles further is a lodge leading up to Plas-y-Bedwellty, an old Mansion. Opposite, on the other side of the river to the right is Woodfield Cottage, the seat of J. Hodder Moggridge, Esq., the proprietor. Argoed, with a good Inn, one and a half miles, and several collieries in the rear. The process of extracting tar from coal may be seen on the opposite side of the river. A little way from the Argoed Inn, on the left, the road turns up a hill, to Bedwellty Church, near which a Roman Causeway leads along the summit towards Tredegar Works. Argoed to Tredegar—six and a half miles.

Mention is made of the uneveness of the road; some early Guides describe them as ditches and the road from Crumlin to Bedwellty and Tredegar, through Croespenmaen, Gwrhay and Argoed was no exception. The good carriage road referred to was, of course, the Turnpike Road, which ran up the valley parallel to the Tramroad. This road ceased to exist when the conversion to a railway was completed in 1860 and Argoed had no road to Tredegar until the new road was built, about 1894. Rather than take the mountain road through Bedwellty to Cefn Golau, Tredegar, many people took a chance and still walked the railway. Mention is also made of extracting tar from coal on the opposite side of the river, which indicates the presence of coke ovens at Gwrhay. The proprietor, at that time, was Roger Lewis, who owned the Coal Level there.

W. W. TASKER

Unrest in the Coal Trade

The first half of the 19th century saw much unrest in the coal trade generally; there was almost a closed shop arrangement with the colliers, and woe betide anyone who worked below the accepted rate for the job. Scotch Cattle and Chartists were very active in the Argoed and Blackwood districts; Croes-pen-maen was a favourite spot for their meetings. Five roads meet at this point and its geographical position is such that it can be reached easily from both the Western and Sirhowy Valleys, including the Pontypool area. Employers gave notice that no Union men would be employed in future. The Union Clubs were crushed, but the Scotch Cattle formed lodges at each colliery.

In January 1830 depression in the Iron Industry forced the price of coal down from 10/- to 8/- a ton, and the colliery companies proposed 2d a ton reduction in wages; but by March 1830 all Monmouthshire workmen were striking for a weekly payment of 10/-, with any balance due, to be paid fortnightly, and for the abolition of the truck system which they hated most. At a mass meeting at Pentwynmawr the owners agreed to keep coal up to a fair market price, to reduce the quantity brought down, and to pay the men in money as proposed. The strike ended on these terms but the management at Manmoel, Cwrt-y-bela and Barnes Collieries refused to honour the agreement to limit output.

Truck shops were company-owned, and the men were forced to purchase all their requirements, including food and clothing etc., at the company's shop. To make sure of this, many employers issued tokens in lieu of money, which were only changeable at the shop; there were exceptions. Roger Lewis of Gwrhay, and Henry Marsh of Blackwood, paid their men 3/6d for a ten hour day and, as a result, their men were working often when the entire district was out on strike. Travel at night at this time was precarious and unsafe. Warnings were directed to certain people in letters sealed with black wax, and a letter sent to three Argoed colliers who were working under price read:—'O Lord, look on thy situation for you shall be in hell before Monday morning'. A John Wilks, described as a 'long-legged devil' who worked as an agent and surveyor at Argoed received advice to 'Pray to God for mercy'. Several company shops in the Bedwellty and Mynydd-islwyn area were broken into and their ledgers set on fire.

Thomas Thomas, employed at Hafodtrisclawd Colliery, was also found to be working under price and received a visit from the Tarw Scotch. Thomas hid under the bed, but his wife, Joan, came down the stairs to see what was happening and was shot in the elbow. She died later because Thomas did not seek medical attention until it was too late. Edward Morgan was found guilty at Monmouth Assizes and was hanged at Monmouth Gaol on 6th April, 1835.

The Chartist Movement was country-wide—Chartism had its beginnings, initially, in the rural communities such as Carmarthenshire, Brecon-

14

shire, and Montgomeryshire. In 1838 the 'People's Charter' was drawn up in which the demands for reform were classified under six points:—

1. Universal Suffrage
2. Equal Electorial Districts
3. Annual Parliaments
4. Vote by Ballot
5. Abolition of Property Qualification for Election to Parliament
6. Payment of Members of Parliament.

Except for clause 3, the demands today seem reasonable enough, but in 1838 they were considered revolutionary. Their aim was complete secrecy of their plans, so much so, that the 'Monmouthshire Merlin' on Saturday, 2nd November, 1838 published a paragraph declaring with satisfaction that Chartism in Monmouthshire was now extinct!

John Frost, a tailor and draper in Mill Street, was born in 1786 and was considered a respectable tradesman and citizen of Newport; he was Mayor of the Town in 1836 and a Magistrate until March 1839, when he was removed from the Magistracy by the Lord Chancellor because of his involvement and association with the Chartist Movement.

Zephaniah Williams was the son of a local farmer; born at Gwrhay, near Argoed in 1795. About 1820 he married Joan Llewellyn, the daughter of a Machen farmer. It was said he knew the Bible from end to end! Believed to have lived for a short time at Tyr Sais Farm, Argoed before going to Sirhowy in 1828 as a Mineral Agent. When Chartism appeared early in the 19th century he was among the first in the valleys to appreciate the meaning of its six principles. He moved in 1839 to Nantyglo and became Landlord of the 'Royal Oak' at Coalbrookvale. As expected, he was in direct opposition to Crawshay Bailey, the Nantyglo Ironmaster and came face to face with him on more than one occasion.

Attack on the Westgate Hotel, Newport,

4th November, 1839

The Chartists were to meet at 6 p.m. on the 3rd November, but Zephaniah Williams did not arrive until 7 p.m. and found Frost at Blackwood pacing restlessly in front of the 'Coach & Horses'. There was heavy rain and flooding, but the Blackwood Streets were thronged. A shot was fired as a signal to march and the Chartists moved off. All the valley contingents followed the Tramroad down to Ty'n-y-Cwm, near the 'Royal Oak', about six miles from Newport and remained until about 6.30 a.m. on the morning of the 4th of November. On their way into Newport the Blackwood men forced their way into Ty'n-y-Cwm Farm and lit a fire to dry their clothes while the farmer, Thomas Saunders, hid in a nearby barn. Later, the combined forces continued down the Tramroad to Pye Corner and Tredegar Park, following the Tredegar Estate Golden Mile until they came to Cwrt-y-bela Farm. Led by Frost, the Chartists advanced up the lane past the Friars to the Turnpike on Stow Hill. Frost then shouted 'Let us go towards the Town and show ourselves to the Town". They knew that Captain Stack had sent Lt. Gray, with two sergeants and twenty-eight privates to the Westgate Hotel; they made that their target. Thomas Phillips, the Mayor, and others had gathered in the Westgate Hotel with special constables in the front line, when Frost and the Chartists arrived, shouting 'Give us the prisoners' (referring to those seized during the night). 'No, never" was the reply from one constable, and another attempted to grab a Chartist's pike. Windows were broken, pierced by bullets and then Lt. Gray ordered his men to load with ball cartridge. As Gray gave the orders, a shot was fired from outside, wounding the Mayor in the arm and hip. A volley was fired into the crowd and into the passageway leading to the hall, and as this happened the crowd dropped their guns, pikes and mandrils, and fled. Twenty-two bodies were recovered later, including William Faraday of Blackwood. They were buried in the Churchyard of St. Woolos. Warrants were issued for the arrest of the leaders and rewards of £100 offered for their capture.

On the 16th January, 1840, Frost, Williams and Jones were sentenced to be drawn on a hurdle to the place of execution, to be hanged; later the jury recommended the prisoners be treated with mercy and the sentence commuted to one of transportation for life. They later sailed from Spithead in the convict ship 'Mandarin' but were landed at Falmouth because the ship lost her topmast. After repairs the ship proceeded and landed at Tasmania on 30th June, 1840. Frost became a clerk in the commandant's office, Williams a superintendent in the coal mines and Jones was appointed an officer in a boys' prison. A pardon was granted to all three in 1854. Frost returned to Bristol and died in 1877, at the age of ninety-three.

Gwrhay, Cwm Corrwg and Argoed

The main benefactors in the Argoed area in the early days were undoubtedly Thomas Phillips and Roger Lewis. They provided employment for many at their collieries at Manmoel, Cwrt-y-bela and Gwrhay. These collieries were connected with Hall's Road Tramway built by Benjamin Hall in about 1805. His son, also Benjamin Hall (later Lord Llanover), as first Commissioner of Works in 1855 was the minister responsible for the placing of the clock on the tower of the Houses of Parliament, and known universally as Big Ben. The section of Hall's Road from Penar Junction to Manmoel Colliery was opened as a standard gauge railway on 10th March, 1886. Later, in 1910, the line was extended to Markham Colliery.

Sir Benjamin Hall was the creator of the Metropolitan Board of Works and his Act for the Metropolis, passed in 1856 was one of the most important measures for the government of London at that time. Sir Benjamin was raised to the peerage in 1859 and as Lord Llanover fought for the survival of the Welsh language, and also for its use in religious services.

Queen's Award for Bravery

After the attack on the Westgate Hotel in Newport and his consequent injury there, Thomas Phillips was knighted by the Queen for his bravery, and was also invited to dine at Buckingham Palace. He was one of the few people in Monmouthshire, at that time, to be granted the Freedom of the City of London, which he received on 26th February, 1840. Incidentally, it may have been Sir Thomas who brought the name Cwrt-y-bela to the Argoed area for it does not appear on early maps. The Court of Wrangling is one suggested translation, the Coat of the Wolf another, and the name seems to have originated from a farm of that name. This farm, owned by the Morgan family in Newport, was used for the sale and auction of cattle, hence the name. Sir Thomas played an important part in the social activity surrounding Argoed at that time and was associated with the building of both the Cwrt-y-bela school and church. This school was built in 1841 and was the first of the works' schools in Wales to be aided by a parliamentary grant. The cost was given as £1,400, Sir Thomas contributing £700 and the remainder found by the Privy Council Board.

Henry Loftus Munroe and Eliza Munroe, the school's master and mistress, were both thirty years of age when joining and had a joint salary of £90 per annum, with house and garden rent free. The school had assistance of six monitors, and boys who were late for morning attendance had to spend one evening gardening for the master. Workmen employed by Sir Thomas at collieries in the area contributed one penny per week in the pound from their wages towards maintenance of the school. The school had a grant in 1866 for an extension and improvements; Gwillim Jenkins did the additional masonry required, whilst woodwork was carried out by Daniel Jones, a local craftsman. The school was situated about half-way up the hill from Cwm Corrwg bridge to Pen-deri Farm, alongside Hall's Tramroad.

The report of the commissioners of 1847 stated that the Cwrt-y-bela school was the best school building in Monmouthshire, and referred to it as 'a handsome building standing on the banks of a deep ravine which skirts the main road to Tredegar (sic) having three spacious rooms, the two outer of which contain galleries'. Another report stated that it was a handsome building standing on the banks of a deep ravine which skirts the tramroad to Tredegar (sic). Most reports were based on the assumption that the school was alongside the Sirhowy Tramroad whereas, in fact, it was situated alongside Hall's Tramroad (later G.W.R. and B.R.) which runs from a junction near Cross Keys in the Western Valley up through Penar Tunnel to the Manmoel area and later, in 1910, to Markham Colliery as previously stated.

Church services were conducted at the school by the Rev. Rees Jones, until the new church at Cwrt-y-bela was built in 1857. I had the pleasure, a few years ago, of reading the School Log Book—it revealed the sometimes casual, and indeed flexible, way in which a country school functions a hundred or so years ago. Unlike today, time off was given for most local functions, but the total holiday for the year was far less than today. Record is made in June 1901, for instance, of the poor attendance by the children, and although the school started at 9.00 a.m., children came in at any time between 9.00 a.m. and 9.45 a.m.! However, on 6th November, 1901 they did not get a holiday, but were given special lessons on the subject of 'The King's Birthday'.

As the following extracts show, the children did well for time off to attend local functions:—

8th May, 1865	— Few children in attendance on account of Blackwood Fair.
29th May, 1865	— School closes early because of exhausting nature of the weather and drowsiness of the children.
4th Sept., 1865	— Teachers and many children 20 minutes late—there being an accident on the railway nearby.

The railway was Hall's Road, which at that time ran only to Hafodtris-clawd Colliery.

7th Sept., 1868	— Picnic in neighbourhood—children dismissed at 3.00 p.m. The school Drum & Fife Band attended.
27th June, 1903	— Day's holiday on account of the annual Parish Tea Party at Penyfan.
6th Oct., 1903	— School Yard flooded; so decided to send children home.
31st Aug., 1903	— Day's holiday on account of Church Choir outing to Weston-super-Mare.
20th May, 1904	— Owing to Club Outing to Abergavenny and Temperance Fete at Tredegar, there was no school.

The Rev. David Gower followed the Rev. Rees Jones as Vicar at Cwrt-y-bela—both gave religious instruction at the school. A curate at Cwrt-y-bela for some years, was the Rev. Lewis David Richards, brother to Miss Irene Richards of Argoed Genol Farm. Miss Richards is shown in the school log book for 1906 as a minitoress. Some may recall her sister, Nellie, who came

18

around the village on foot with the milk; it was supplied from the Jack in those days, with the customer bringing the jug to the door.

The Committee of Management for the school in 1900 included the following:—

Rev. David Gower,
Mr. Pritchard, Crumlin Hall,
Mr. Thomas, Cwrt-y-bela,
Rev. S. W. Williams, Newbridge,
Mr. John Powell, Gwrhay Fawr,
Mr. Lewis Williams, Penmaen,
Mr. Morgan, Llwynon.

Crumlin Hall was built by Mr. Kennard, the designer of Crumlin Viaduct, and from the upstairs windows of the Hall he could see the day-to-day progress in the construction of the Viaduct. In later years the Hall was taken over by D. F. Pritchard, who established a brewery at Crumlin. He was chairman for some years of Bedwellty Show but later moved to Goytre Hall, near Abergavenny. Crumlin Hall later became a Mining & Technical College, but afterwards demolished.

Cwrt-y-bela Church

The church at Cwrt-y-bela is dedicated to the Saints Phillip and James—the surname of Sir Thomas and of his wife's maiden name. The first minister, the Rev. Rees Jones lived at Myrtle Grove, Blackwood and, to give better access to the new church, bridges were erected over the Sirhowy Railway and the river opposite Gwrhay, but there was probably some sort of river bridge there long before this. The railway bridge (now demolished) quickly became known as the 'Parson's Bridge'—a name time has failed to eradicate! In railway records it was simply Bridge No. 26—indicating that it was the twenty-sixth bridge on the railway from Nantybwch. The first bridge, built of wood, had the steps in line with the bridge itself, and was erected by the Sirhowy Railway Company, whereas the bridge, as we knew it last, before the railway was closed, was built by the London & North Western Railway.

Sir Thomas was a Queen's Councillor of the Inner Temple, but in later years relinquished his practice as a barrister and devoted his life to business and social activities and gave endless assistance to the poor of Newport, in many cases paying fines for them at the Courts, as the following amusing extract from the 'Monmouthshire Merlin' on the 20th February, 1840 shows:—

'Mary—a poor old Irish widow whose rental was below two shillings per week came forward at Newport Police Court, in compliance with a summons from the overseers, and stated, with a rich accent, that her cabin was situated in Fothergill-street, and "hersel' and five blessed childer" were all who occupied it. She was a poor, lone widow, and she hoped their "werchips" would not make her pay the "same rint to the oversare!" Sir Thomas Phillips told the poor old creature she would not have to pay the rate. Dropping a most profound curtsey, she joyfully exclaimed "Thankee, ye werchip, I and sure, isn't it mysel' that'll pray for ye all my life long".'

His untimely death came whilst addressing a committee meeting at Gloucester Place in London on Tuesday, 21st May, 1867, and he was buried near his mother and father at Llanelly, Breconshire; he was sixty-six years of age. Sir Thomas never forgot his association with the School at Argoed, and gave talks each year to the children at the Annual Festival and Examinations in August. The elite of the neighbourhood attended these functions. In 1866, for instance, those present included Mrs. Bond, Tredegar; Matthew Ion, Rhoswen Farm, Argoed; Captain and Miss Williams, Maesrudded; Sir Thomas Phillips and the Rev. Leigh and Family, Bedwellty. Mrs. Bond was the wife of Mr. Robert Bond, the manager of the Sirhowy Railway Company. Funeral services were conducted at Cwrt-y-bela Church by the Rev. Rees Jones; the congregation came from far and wide, and many were unable to gain entry to the service. Sir Thomas's father had been manager at one time of the Llanelly Works near Abergavenny and his brother, Mr. B. Phillips, was an eminent surgeon.

Roger Lewis of Gwrhay bought the Gwrhay Level and Coke Ovens in 1848, he died at his residence, Penmaen House in December 1874 at the age of eighty-three; he was one of the oldest and most respected members of the South Wales Coal Trade. Many years later, Mrs. Miriam Lewis of Gwrhay Fach Farm was the proprietor of the Gwrhay Level. Like Cwm Corrwg at Argoed, there was much activity at the Gwrhay before the villages of Argoed and Blackwood came into being; the place abounded with levels and air shafts, mostly connected to the Mynddislwyn and Brithdir coal seams. At the southern end of Gwrhay, the Tredegar Iron Company drove a heading in 1815 and it was named Waterloo after the battle of that name.

The name Barnes had associations with the Gwrhay area in the 1830s, and in more recent years a lease was granted to William Barnes for the working of Islwyn Colliery, behind Cwrt-y-bela and I well remember, as a boy, being shown a stationary steam engine and horizontal boiler which, I presume, worked a fan or compressor there.

Other small collieries on the Mynyddislwyn side of the river were Woodfield and Týr Philkins.

The Woodfield Colliery was owned by Thomas Prothero of Malpas Court, Newport. In 1842 he employed fifty-nine adults, four under eighteen years of age and one under thirteen. Two men and two boys were engaged at pumping. Many would not have heard of this colliery were it not for the publicity in the local press concerning the falling of the boiler-house stack in 1872. Erected in 1831, it was reputed to contain nearly 1,000,000 bricks and to be one of the highest stacks in South Wales.

The major problem was that there were two rows of houses near at hand. Great credit was due to the colliery manager of the time, Mr. Temple Stroud, for the careful and skilful way in which the operation was carried out. In three minutes the whole mass was levelled to the ground in the exact position required. Mr. Stroud was a lieutenant in the Blackwood Volunteers, but later gave up his post as colliery manager to become a tenant farmer at Cwmbyrnar Farm, Mynddislwyn. The local farmers welcomed him by, on a given day, supplying teams of horses, gaily decorated, to plough all the land. The evening concluded with a dinner and plenty of liquid refreshment. After dinner the toast of the day was 'Success to Lt. Stroud as Tenant Farmer' which was received with tremendous cheering.

Woodfield Colliery was sited across the river almost opposite Libanus, Blackwood, whereas the new Woodfield Colliery was situated much higher up near the Rhiw, where the G.W.R. carried out further accommodation sidings in 1909. In 1870 Tŷr Philkins Colliery had its own tramway system, and a steam-driven fan and haulage and employed 49 workmen. The new pits were opened in 1874, celebrated by a grand dinner for all sinkers, mechanics and engineers connected with the Works; this was laid on at the 'Royal Oak', Blackwood. The colliery suffered extensive flooding at various times and in 1877, 150 men and boys were out for three weeks because of this. Tŷr Philkins was owned by Henry and Walter Powell, sons of Thomas Powell of the Gaer, Newport.

Although Hall's Road branch was essentially a mineral line, taking coal from all the collieries from Markham right down to Tŷr Philkins at one time, many will be surprised to learn that as from 14th March, 1927, a passenger service (auto-train) ran from Oakdale and Penmaen Halts to Pontypool Road and back. Oakdale Halt closed in 1932 and the service ceased from Penmaen Halt on 25th September, 1939.

Rock Chapel

Rock Chapel was founded in 1824, with approximately twenty-five members; but before this there was a meeting house on the corner, at the bottom of the hill. Evan Jones, the chief deacon, was born in the district of Llangeitho, Cardiganshire on 17th June, 1802, and together with John Jones of Gwrhay, also a deacon, formed the mainstay in the early development of the Calvinistic Cause at the Rock. Before this, John Jones attended Penmaen Chapel, but later went to Gelligroes, a four mile walk. In 1818 he married Leah Williams, daughter of Walter Williams of Cwrt-y-bela who was also a member of Gelligroes. In 1824 they both attended Rock. He was a Sunday School Teacher for fifty-eight years, a member with the Calvinistic Methodists for forty-eight years and a deacon for thirty-three years. He died on 23rd September 1863.

The Rector of Bedwellty at that time was also a native of Llangeitho and had heard of Evan Jones, whom, he thought, may be the man he was looking for to teach at Bedwellty School where educational facilities were poor. In 1847 Evan Jones was invited to take the post at a salary of 7/6d (37.1/2 p) per week. To supplement his meagre earnings, Evan's mother agreed to supply him with cheese, butter and meat for the first five years and the Rector and his family gave all the assistance they could.

The children at Bedwellty were rude and unruly at times and frequently Evan Jones had to leave them to their own devices and resort to prayer in the church tower!

William Jones (Asaph Gwent) lived at Gwrhay, but it seems his presence at Rock Chapel was not welcome and it was said that he gave no help to the cause there.

In 1900 there were four deacons at Rock and communicants, including minister, preachers, deacons and other members totalled sixty-two. One hundred and fifty-two were in the habit of attending regularly, including fifty-two members of the Band of Hope, ten teachers and officers and sixty-four scholars. The chapel could seat four hundred. Morning services were conducted in Welsh and in the evening in English. The chapel secretary was W. J. Harris of Argoed Farm and the organist, Mrs. Davies.

Only once can I remember Rock Chapel filled to capacity, with chairs in the aisles, and this was during a visit by Dr. Martin Lloyd-Jones in the early 1930s. From another source comes the fact that Madame Adelina Patti, the celebrated Italian singer came from Craig-y-nos Castle to sing at a concert at Rock Chapel, and also that 'Islwyn' (William Thomas) the Welsh poet from Ynysddu preached at Rock on several occasions.

Some of the members at Rock in 1900 or before included:—

John Williams—Cwmgelly	Margaret Jenkins—Argoed
Sarah Williams—Cwmgelly	Mary Price—Waterloo
Robert Howells—Argoed (Stationmaster)	Margaret Hascol—Cottage
	Mrs. Price—Argoed Mill
David Evans—Gwrhay	William Williams—Waterloo
William Duggins—Argoed	William Moses—Twyn Simon
Henry Thomas—Rock	Mary Powell—Twyn Simon
David Morgan—Argoed	Ann Hopkin—Darrenfelin
Lewis Price—Ty'r Capel	Amelia Lewis—Darrenfelin
Evan Jones—Bedwellty	Edmund Evans—Pontygwaith
Watkin Rodrick—Rock Shop	Mrs. Jenkins—Argoed Shop
Rachel Walters—Argoed	Mary Powell—
Sarah Pugh—Pencoed	Woodfield Lodge
Mary Price—Gwrhay	Mary Jones—Tyr Graig
Rebecca Price—Gwrhay	Margaret Rees—Myrtlegrove
Mrs. Bethel—Argoed	Margaret Gwylym
Leah Jones—Gwrhay	Jenkins—Argoed
Jacob Williams—Coaltar	Thomas Powell—Gelli Shop

Before leaving the Mynyddislwyn area and Gwrhay, mention may be made of local inhabitants of the past. Mr. and Mrs. Workman lived at

Cwrt-y-bela Crossing House—he was in the Permanent Way Maintenance Gang, and his wife, the Crossing Keeper. Mr. Workman attended morning service at Bedwellty Church, passing up Sunny View at Argoed; he never failed to pass the time of day, and often stopped for a friendly chat; he was a keen gardener. He sometimes returned home through the Cwm, quite a trip for a nonagenarian. Another Gwrhay resident was Mrs. Wyatt, of Waterloo Cottages (now demolished) who celebrated her one hundredth birthday in June 1935.

The Rock

The Rock Inn was used extensively for Parish Meetings and Petty Sessions for the Bedwellty District, including the registration of voters and the collection of tithes. All petty theft and accidents on the tramroad and at collieries was dealt with here. J.P.s, at various times, were Captain Marsh, Captain Williams and T. Llewellyn Brewer, G. T. James, William Llewellyn and Edmund Leigh (Rector of Bedwellty). An 1860 map of the district depicts what appears to be a building in the roadway, and from information handed down over the years, gates were placed across the road at night.

The following extracts appeared in the 'Monmouthshire Merlin' for 8th September, 1849:—

> Registration of Voters. County of Monmouth.
> At the Rock Inn, on Wednesday, September 19th 1849 at 11 o'clock forenoon for the Parishes of:—
>> Aberystwyth
>> Bedwas Higher & Lower
>> Bedwellty
>> Llanhilleth
>> Mynddislwyn

The area covered was quite extensive. Local influential people shown on an agreement to construct a footpath between Blackwood and Argoed in 1858 included the following:—

> Sirhowy Tramroad. on the one part, and
> William Davies, of Canton. Parish of Llandaff.
> William Williams, Maesruddud, Blackwood.
> Edward Davies, Woodbine Cottage, Parish of Bedwellty.
> Surgeon George Lewis.
> William Jones, Blackwood.
> E. D. Williams, Maesruddud, Blackwood.
> Aneurin Jones (Anuerin Fardd), Gelligroes. Miller.
> John Jones, Rock House, Blackwood.
> James George James, Tynewydd, Argoed.

Mrs. Esau of Oakdale recalls that her grandfather, William Morgan, the blacksmith, had his workshop on the corner at the bottom of the hill leading to Bedwellty, but later moved to the other side of the public house where the present garage is now. Mr. Morgan was also the innkeeper for a time: but Jeremiah Price, who was proprietor in 1877, was charged for keeping his house open for sale of beer on Sunday and consequently fined 10/- and costs.

There was a brew house at the back of the Inn. Watkin Watkins worked as a wheelwright, with John Dalby (smith) in the 1850s. Much later, Fred Meredith traded as carpenter and wheelwright.

Early maps record the existence of a corn mill near the river bridge at the Rock.

Argoed buildings at the Rock (old white-washed houses in blocks of four, now demolished) built in the Sirhowy Tramroad days, were occupied by porters, signalmen, and platelayers and during the 1920s as many as six signalmen were living there.

In the small gap between these blocks of four there was an Irish settlement housing navvies working on the construction of the Sirhowy Tramroad; in the early tramroad days horses were changed from stables at the Rock which were situated opposite the Blackwood end of Rock Villas. Lower down, opposite the colliery was Walter Bevan's shop, named 'Rhoswen Shop', from the colliery of that name above Argoed, owned at that time by Bevan & Pryce. Walter Bevan married Harriet Ellis, a daughter of Thomas Ellis of Tredegar, the Engineer to the Sirhowy Tramroad Company; she was one of Mr. Ellis's eleven children. The shop was leased from the Sirhowy Railway Company for seventy-nine years from 1851. During the Chartists' uprising, desperadoes broke into the house of Mr. Thomas Rees, shopkeeper at the Rock, breaking all the furniture and tried to fire the bedroom in which Mr. and Mrs. Rees slept; fortunately they failed. There were several barrels of gunpowder on the premises, used for shot-firing underground. Gunpowder was stored in small magazines under lock and key by all the small levels which were scattered all over the area.

Before the shops became numerous, tradesmen called regularly at houses with their wares or services. Colliers and ironworkers needed strong clothes, and Mr. Morgan Jones of Ty-Newydd Cottage, Bedwellty provided just what they wanted. 'The Stocking Man' as he was known locally, carried a wooden frame on his shoulder—this had wooden rails on which were displayed long woollen stockings for men, working shirts, woollens of various kinds, and rolls of Welsh flannel in grey, red and white from factories at Maesycwmmer, Blackwood and Argoed, and even Carmarthenshire. The business was carried on by his son, Mr. Jenkin Jones at Argoed Post Office, and is still going as a family business by his son, Myrddin Jones.

The tinsmith, Sam Jones, made household equipment for all purposes—bread and cake tins, Dutch ovens for fixing in front of the kitchen fire and toasting forks, etc. He came once a month, with all the necessary gear—

tinplate, wire, solder and flux, and needed a good kitchen fire for heating his soldering iron!

'Scissors to Grind' was a cry we often heard years ago. The grindstone was fixed on a wooden frame with wheels, with pedal-drive for the revolving stone. Housewives needed sharp knives and men then used the open cut-throat razors.

The Rock Colliery

There were two headings at the Rock. One was almost behind the Inn and the other near Rock Villas. The heading near the Villas was named 'Primrose' by Christopher Pond. The colliery screens were situated on the roadside, and behind the screens was a vertical, twin-cylinder haulage engine which was extremely noisy when working hard. The railway siding ran across the main road and the full wagons were dropped across and picked up by the train engine. A horse was kept in a stable on the other side of the railway where the colliery refuse was tipped. This was reached by a tramway across the road and under the railway. Looking at the site now, it is difficult to realise that the colliery screens and wagons were only a few yards from the road traffic. Love & Gittins were the proprietors before its closure in the 1950s.

During 1946-53 I saw many private owner wagons at Rock, including G.L.M., Manchester Collieries and Barrow & Barnsley Main Collieries.

Number employed. 1910, 75.
Number employed. 1916, 47, underground. 8 above.

Collieries at Gwaelodywain, Penyfan, and Yr-ochor-with at Ynysddu were worked by Christopher Pond.

Journey through the Cwm to Argoed

The Rev. Rees Jones journeyed from Myrtle Grove, Blackwood, (near the top of Foundry Hill) to the new church at Cwrt-y-bela each Sunday in the 1860s. We can now follow in his footsteps over the Parson's Bridge, down sharply to the river and up on to the railway crossing at Cwrt-y-bela, turning left along the Cwm road to Cwm Corrwg; once over the Bridge 'Pont Cwm Corrwg', (shown as 'Pont Sir Powell' on early maps), we are back in the Parish of Bedwellty standing on, possibly, one of the oldest sites in the Sirhowy Valley.

Dora Williams' father had a small lock-up shop at one time on the Cwm road where he sold fish. It was brought from Argoed Station in a hand cart. Just before crossing the river bridge, a road leads up to the right, under

Hall's Road railway, where some years ago, on the left, stood Cwrt-y-bela School. Beyond was Collier's Row, a block of five old houses, occupied at one time by colliers in the area. Further up the hill is Pen-deri Farm. The buildings in the Cwm could be divided into two sections—the original stone buildings on the west bank of the river and the new houses erected in the 20th century, each side of the river. Buildings on the west bank consisted of the main Flannel Factory building and structures immediately behind and also the Corn Mill, which was probably the oldest building there. It is, indeed, unfortunate that the Flannel Factory and the Mill were demolished—they would have made perfect examples of early industry in the valley. When they actually started making Welsh Flannel in the Cwm is difficult to ascertain but 'Slater's 1850 Directory' mentions Catherine John, William Price and Thomas Tuck as Woollen Manufacturers, and according to early ordnance survey maps, water to the factory came from the Mill Race. The Sluice Gate on the river was opposite Argoed Railway Station.

The Corn Mill is referred to as 'that tenement with the Water Corn Grist Mill, called Mellin Yr Argoed Ucha' also 'that Corn or Malt Kiln'. The oldest record I can find is a Rent Valuation Roll of Thomas Morgan for the collection of rents for the year 1698 when the rent due was just £1. The Mill underwent major repairs in 1848, and again in 1869 when the masonry was done by Gwillim Jenkins. Farmers in the district gathered here and no doubt, it was a focal point for all the local gossip. The Mill owners used the old Store House situated alongside the railway for the storage of grain. The Mill Race came under the Cwm Road and divided opposite the main factory building, one to the woollen factory and the other to the corn mill. In 'Kelly's Directory' for 1890, the factory was known as the 'Argoed Welsh Flannel Factory Ltd.', and in 'Lascelles County Directory' for 1852 mention is made of Eliza James, beer retailer and woollen manufacturer, Cymreigyddion House, Argoed, which is believed to have been at the back of the main factory building, and near to where, in later years, Mr. Gomer Hughes had his shop. It seems that the corn mill was rented from E. D. Williams, Maesruddud and had various occupants—William Price of the Castle Public House, David Hopkins, James Walters, John Walters and many others.

Interestingly, the Welsh flannel liquid dye was collected around the houses each morning in pails which were carried by means of yokes placed over the person's shoulders!

Eliza James was the wife of Evan James, who wrote the words of the Welsh National Anthem, 'Hen Wlad Fy Nhadau'. He was born in the parish of Eglwysilian on the 14th October, 1809. About 1813 the family moved to Cwm Corrwg, Argoed, where he was a weaver at the flannel factory, and also the proprietor of a beer house situated in a part of the old houses between the factory and the river bridge as previously mentioned. Evan was well-known by his bardic name 'Ieuan ap Iago' and devoted much of his time to reading and discussing of Welsh literature, and also to the composition of Welsh verse. He and his son, James, jointly wrote a number of songs; one the words, and the other the music, but 'Hen Wlad fy Nhadau' seems to be the only one published.

According to an article by Mr. Daniel Huws in 'The National Library of Wales Journal' (Vol. XVI No. 2) for 1969, Evan James married in about 1832, and his wife, Elizabeth, gave birth to two sons, James in 1833 and Daniel in 1835. There were also five other children by the marriage. It was his son, James, who composed the music for the Welsh National Anthem in 1856 while living at Pontypridd. In contrast, Mr. R. W. Davies, a Pontypridd Borough Librarian, indicates that James James was born on 4th November, 1832 at the Ancient Druid Inn, Hollybush; and so there is a variation in the birth date and the whereabouts of the family at that time.

There is little doubt that while writing his poems, Evan was carried away with the life and beauty of the Sirhowy Valley and the mill, and of Cwm Crach in particular. Many in Argoed today would not know where Cwm Crach is—the dingle runs parallel to the Bedwellty road at the top of Sunny View and extended originally down to the Cwm and the river. Due to the Cwm Crach workings, refuse was strewn all over the place; consequently the beauty of the brook (Nant Crach) and the dingle of former years is no longer with us. To recreate the scene one must forget the railway and the new main road. The late Edmund Williams, born in Argoed in the 1850s, told me that the district was known as the Crachan years ago.

Teithiasom ni ganwaith yn araf o'r glyn
I'r hen ysgol wledig dros glogwyn y bryn
Cydoedi, cydchwareu nes byddem mewn braw
O'n cospi gan fedwen ein meistr rhag llaw.
   Clyd ydoedd ei breswyl oleuwyd drwy'r dellt
   Tan gysgod y dderwen, y bwthyn to gwellt.

Pan ddeuai dydd Sadwrn y cyfleu a gaem
Am bysgod i afon Sirhowy yr aem,
Cydredeg mewn hyder at odreu Cwm Gwrach
A phob un a'i linyn, abwydyn a bach
   Clyd &

Cydchwareu a'r man-blant y buom cyn hyn
Wrth hen ffwrn y felin ar waelod y glyn,
Pan fyddai ymryson a brwydrau er gwall
Mor fawr y cynhyrfem y naill dros y llall
   Clyd &

[We travelled a hundred times slowly from the vale
to the old rural school over the crag of the hill,
Hanging around and playing together until we would be afraid
of being punished by our master's birch.
   Snug was his dwelling that was lit through the laths
   under the shadow of the oak, the cottage with a thatched roof.

> When Saturday came we would have the opportunity
> to go to the Sirhowy river for fish,
> We'd run together confidently to the foot of Cwm Gwrach
> each one with his line, bait and hook.
>   Snug &

> We had played together with the small children before this
> by the mill's old store at the bottom of the vale,
> When there were competitions and struggles, despite defeat
> how excited we would become one for the other.
>   Snug &]

James James was an ardent music lover and an accomplished harpist and singer, and assisted his father in his business at Pontypridd and later, in the year 1873, went to live at Mountain Ash, where he was the host of the Collier's Arms Inn, remaining there until 1891. The closing years of Iago ap Ieuan were spent at Aberdare and he died at 6 Hawthorne Terrace on 11th January, 1902, and was buried at Aberdare Cemetery.

A well informed account of the composition of the melody is provided by Taliesin James, one of James James' five children, in a letter by him dated 4th December, 1910, to John Crockett of Pontypridd who used to teach James James harp playing. This letter, now in the Cardiff Central Public Library, reads, in parts, as follows:—

> 'I have often heard my father say that on a Sunday afternoon in that month and year (January 1856) he went for a walk up the Rhondda Road and that the melody came into his mind. Returning to my grandfather's house, but a few doors from his own, he said to him, 'Father, I have composed a melody which is in my opinion a very fitting one for a Welsh patriotic song. Will you write some verses for it? "Let me hear it", said my grandfather, then he said, "Fetch your harp, James". My father brought the harp to the Factory House and played the air on that instrument. My grandfather was greatly struck with it, and at once took down his slate, which, I daresay you know, always hung by the side of his armchair by the fireplace, and in a few minutes the words of the first verse were written. The second and third verses were written the next day'.

The original manuscript of the words and melody, in the writing of James James, is to be found in a book of manuscript music which belonged to him and is now in the National Library of Wales, Aberystwyth.

Another account of how 'Hen Wlad fy Nhadau' came to be composed appears in 'The Story of the National Anthem of Wales' by Sir Alfred T. Davies:—

> 'Evan James (Ieuan ap Iago, to give him the bardic title by which he was best known among his poetaster contemporaries) was a weaver by trade. Like many a Welshman, whether weaver, shoe-maker, or shepherd, he mixed poetry with his work. On the following (Sunday)

morning he caused a message to be sent to his son James (Iago ap Ieuan) asking him to come to him and bring with him his harp. Accordingly, in the evening, "when the people were in chapel", and his son, nothing loth, "slipped down to his father's house" where later, on her return home his mother—finding him there with his beloved instrument, and doubtless playing it—sharply rebuked him. The rejoinder which she thereby brought upon herself, and which related to a certain Biblical incident connected with David and his harp, seemingly closed further discussion on the subject, else the result might, perhaps, have been less happy for the world than, fortunately, proved to be the case.

And so, it came about in this simple way and on that Sunday evening, whilst the father held in his hand the slate on which he was wont to jot down the thoughts which had surged through his mind during the day, the son swept the strings of his harp to the notes of the now imperishable melody which came to him as he did so. The older man, carefully adapting his words to the air, gave utterance to the theme which now forms part of the heritage of Welsh people everywhere. Neither father nor son, in obedience to some overpowering influence, could free himself from the spell of the national sentiment which each wished to express. The song and the air are inseparably connected; they issued together as twins from the womb of thought. The first verse of "Land of my Fathers" was finished that night; the second and third verses were added "by early dawn of the next day". Such is the simple story of the original of the melody which its composers named "Cwm (sic) Rhondda".'

The accounts leave us somewhat bewildered. Leaving aside the less important question as to whether the collaboration of father and son occurred on a Saturday or a Sunday evening, and whether beer was employed as a stimulus to poetic inspiration.

(This account is based upon an article in the 'Dictionary of Welsh Biography' by Henry Blackwell, of New York, now in the National Museum of Wales (N.L.W. MSS. 9251-77.)

And yet another explanation, as to the origins of our National Anthem, comes from Owen Morgan (Morien) in his 'History of Pontypridd and Rhondda Valleys', (1903). The information he says came from the poet himself and is reproduced below:—

' "It was" said the Bard "on a Sunday evening, in January 1856. My wife and some of the children had gone to the service at Carmel Chapel and I was quite alone. I had been brooding over thrilling incidents in the past history of Wales. My age at the time was 46 and James my eldest son was 24 years old, and he played excellently on the harp. I had gone upstairs, intending to retire early, and was partly undressed when I heard James entering the house and then calling out, 'Yn Nhad, dewch i lawr yn union!' (Father come down immediately!)

29

The harper spoke so excitedly that I went down as I was". "I have been", said James "for a stroll along the side of the river Rhondda, and in the sound of its roar I have composed a new melody which has greatly moved me". "His face was aglow" said the father. The father invited his son to play it on his harp. The harp of Wales was brought forth to the middle of the room, then "Among the strings his fingers strayed" and with closed eyes the young Kimmerian sought to recall the notes which the dancing waters of the Rhondda River had suggested to his soul. While thus engaged the mother returned from Mount Carmel conventicle and cried to James, "What in the world is the meaning of this! Playing the harp on the Sunday night!" "Mam anwyl", replied James, "Don't forget King David played the harp of the tribe of royal Judah in the house of the Lord". Then the young harper of the Rhondda River bank caught the immortal strain and the mother and father looked entranced.'

HEN WLAD FY NHADAU

Mae hen wlad fy nhadau yn annwyl i mi,
Gwlad beirdd a chantorion, enwogion o fri;
Ei gwrol ryfelwyr, gwladgarwyr tra mad,
   Tros ryddid gollasant eu gwaed.

   Gwlad, gwlad, pleidiol wyf i'm gwlad;
   Tra môr yn fur, i'm bur hoff bau,
   O bydded i'r hen iaith barhau.

Hen Gymru fynyddig paradwys y bardd,
Pob dyffryn, pob clogwyn, i'm golwg sy'n hardd:
Trwy dennlad gwladgarol, mor swynol yw si
   Ei nentydd, afonydd, i fi.

   Gwlad, gwlad, pleidiol wyf i'm gwlad;
   Tra môr yn fur, i'm bur hoff bau,
   O bydded i'r hen iaith barhau.

Os treisiodd y gelyn fy ngwlad dan ei droed,
Mae hen iaith y Cymry mor fyw ag erioed:
Ni luddiwyd yr awen gan erchyll law brad,
   Na thelyn bereiniol fy ngwlad.

   Gwlad, gwlad, pleidiol wyf i'm gwlad;
   Tra môr yn fur, i'm bur hoff bau,
   O bydded i'r hen iaith barhau.

Pontypridd

English Translation by Eben Fardd

The land of my fathers, the land of my choice.
The land in which poets and minstrels rejoice:

The land whose stern warriors were true to the core,
While bleeding for freedom of yore.

Wales! Wales! favourite land o' Wales!
While sea her wall, may nought befall
To mar the old language of Wales.

In the early part of this century additional houses were erected in the Cwm—some, I believe, were built by George Doidge. Island Street got its name because of its situation, between the river and the Mill Race, in fact, almost all the original Cwm buildings were on the Island! Other streets were Upper and Lower James Street (probably named after George James, Glangrwyney) and Greenfield Terrace. Sam Haines had his grocer's shop at one end of Island Street. In more recent times, Mr. and Mrs. Rowe had a sweets and newsagents business in James Street.

Incidentally, a Baptism was held in the Sirhowy River at Cwm Corrwg in 1811.

Argoed Village

Passing the Castle Public House on the right, we face the very steep hill, with the old storehouse up high on the left, used years ago by those occupying the mill; nearby was Charlotte's House, long disappeared. Before going under the railway arch into Argoed Village, there was a sweet shop owned by Mrs. Ayres—it was out of bounds for us, but occasionally items like those long thin bands of liquorice were a half-penny cheaper there and no time was lost in cashing in on the deal! Gob-stoppers were sometimes cheaper!

The village is now a mere shadow of its former self—the character of it changed for the worse with the building of the new Argoed Arms Hotel— completely out of keeping with the rest of the buildings, especially when viewed from the rear. The village was once a pleasant and fairly busy place, with enough shops to make it almost self-contained. These shops gradually disappeared as more people travelled to Blackwood for their shopping, and the closing of the collieries in the district induced some of the younger families to move.

I remember many who lived in the village—the Revd John Jenkins, white-bearded, he never failed to speak, and Edwin Jenkins, busily brushing the front of his shop in the morning, working that false hand of his around the corners; he was about early too, and invariably stopped me in the mornings when catching the 7.40 a.m. train. Jim and Emily Phillips were real characters. A haircut with Jim could take up to half an hour with him trotting to the shop counter at frequent intervals; though come to think of it, trotting was probably out of the question—Mr. Phillips had a club foot!

At the Post Office was Mr. Jenkin Jones and Louisa Jones, followed by

Mr. and Mrs. Harold Weaver, and at the other end of the village, David Morgan, the ironmonger, where the Co-op was later. Jediah Thomas was our butcher who made his own sausages; his machine, at the back of his premises, always fascinated me. He retired on Saturday, 5th December, 1936. How many readers remember Ernie Williams, the lamp-lighter, who lived at 14 High Street, Argoed (now demolished). His last lamp was at the bottom of the hill going down from the Rock, near Rhiw Syr Dafydd bridge, and the old cottage on the right (again, now demolished).

What a wonderful shop Argoed Shop was in its original form (it was known as Argoed Shop by all). I can only remember it towards the end, but I can recall seeing Nest Jenkins, usually at the desk on the left-hand side entering the shop; and also recall Elizabeth Jenkins, who assisted in the Bakehouse where a lot of cake-making went on, especially at Whitsun for the Sunday School treats and parties. We took our own pies, tarts, etc., for baking there.

Early in 1929—at a time when the baker (Mr. Huish, who worked all night at the bakehouse) and myself used to catch the morning train down (he lived at Pontllanfraith), P.C. Amphlett caught an intruder getting into the sweet shop of Renee Powles, near the garage, in the early hours of the morning. He proved to be a bigger man than Amphlett and a fierce struggle took place, but he was eventually handcuffed to a part of the machinery in the bakehouse—the only place open at that hour of the morning. P.C. Amphlett lost his helmet, found later near the Argoed Signal Box, and his tunic was torn in the struggle. I often wonder if the baker got his mix right that morning and the bread out on time.

In the old days wagons of coal, coke and flour were dropped down from the station yard to Argoed Shop, and horses pulled the vehicles when empty back to the yard. The room at the back of the shop was used for cheese and bacon, cut from the flitch, and the tea, which came in large chests was packeted at the shop. A cellar underneath the back room was used for storage. Fortunately, pre-packaged foods and additives had not arrived then. The shop had a box cart and the driver, John Edwards, sat on top. When not in use, the cart was stored in a building alongside Jim, the barber. 'Lascelles Directory' for 1852 mentions Isaac Jenkins, Grocer and Draper, Argoed. The business was clearly well-established, and one of the earliest in Argoed and the district around. Isaac Jenkins was, no doubt, the founder of the business, he died on 18th November, 1893. The shop was taken over later by Brinley Jenkins, and finally by Emlyn John. Few will remember John Jones, Cabinet Maker (who also made Coffins). A fine craftsman; his father, Daniel Jones, was also in the trade, and is recorded in 'Slater's' 1850 and 1880 Directories. Some may recall David Meredith—grocer, who kept the shop, still standing on the New Road, between the 'Prims' Chapel and the Mission Hall. It has now been converted into a house. The old Cwm Crach Tramroad ran alongside the house on its way from the Level at the top, under the new road to screens on the side of the railway.

'Kelly's Directory' for 1910 included George Doidge, builder of Argoed. I believe he built Sunny View, Woodville, Golynos Avenue and George Street, in that alpine setting—perhaps the last mentioned was named after him.

The Post Office

In September, 1891 a meeting was held with Mr. H. L. Munroe, (son of the old schoolmaster) in the chair, and it was agreed to discuss with the Postmaster at Newport, the possibility of establishing a Post Office at Argoed. However, four months later, no decision had been reached. (Blackwood was the nearest Post Office at the time). By 1900 Edward Lewis was Sub-Postmaster at Argoed, and by 1905, Elizabeth Margaret Evans (Margaret Charles) had taken over as Postmistress.

In September of that year, the local paper reported the following:—

'Great changes are taking place in the neighbourhood of Argoed—new collieries are being opened, and new roads are being made, and numerous houses are being built. Hundreds of workmen have been drafted into the place—Argoed is no longer a silent and deserted village'.

Abernant Colliery had recently been sunk and the new road from Tredegar to Argoed was about to be commenced. There was already a narrow road for most of the way to Blackwood, which had been completed at the time of the conversion of the tramway to a railway, but part of it remained as a footpath for a time.

The Argoed of the 1860s had a public house, but this was on the opposite side of the road to the present one and, when it was demolished, a lodging house, run by a Mr. Morgan was built on the site. Near the corner of the road leading up to the New Road, stood a reading room and library. It was known as Ebly's, but I believe his real name may have been Ebenezer Lewis; he had spent some time in America; later he came to the Mill in the Cwm where it was said he applied graphite to the Mill bearings when overheating occurred.

During a sale of property in 1900, numbers 19, 20 and 21, High Street, Argoed, let to Messrs. D. Thomas, Elias Smith & J. Perkins were described as 'being near the station and having excellent gardens stocked with fruit trees'. To be near the station in those days was a real asset as road transport did not exist. In the 1880s further houses were erected at Fairoak, including those at Grwyney Terrace and Grwyney Place for George James of Glangrwyney, near Crickhowell. He owned the Board Mills there and was associated, at one time, with the Flannel Factory in the Cwm. A new section of road from the north end of the village, near the station, to the new road was completed in June 1926 and opened by Councillor Clifford Thomas. The contract price was £4,770 but eventually cost £4,600, an impossibility today!

Prior to this, there were very steep steps, leading to a black ash path which entered the main Tredegar Road by the top gate of the junior school, and in September 1926, a new infants' school was opened at Argoed by Councillor Panes at a cost of £8,487.

The 'South Wales Argus' reported in July 1926 that a grant of £2,000 had enabled the Welfare Council to push forward work in connection with the New Miners' Institute at Argoed. A building adjoining the Argoed Arms Hotel had been purchased and it was planned that this would house a billiard hall, library and concert hall.

Sunday School Marches

The Baptists and Primitive Methodists joined forces for the annual Whit Monday march, then had tea at the Chapels. Afterwards everyone spent an enjoyable afternoon in a field, kindly made available by Mrs. E. L. Jenkins of Argoed Farm. Leading the singing in the afternoon was Lew Roberts, Joseph Jones and William Dodd. Childrens' races were organised, with prizes for the lucky ones. Later, in the evening, the favourite game with the adults was 'Kiss in the Ring'. A large outer ring of females enclosed a smaller ring inside of males.

The two rings rotated in opposite directions singing:—

> There was a farmer had a dog
> His name was Bobby Bingo
> Bingo, Bingo, Bingo
> His name was Bobby Bingo.

After the chant, the six males selected six females and gracefully kissed them!

The Argoed Arms had a good name for catering and many societies and associations held their annual dinners there. On 29th January, 1870, the Hunt from Cefn Crib (Mr. Herberts) held their dinner there when over sixty sat down to a feast. Richard Evans was the proprietor at the time, before him Mary Lloyd was the host. Tragically she was killed on Monday, 23rd August, 1858 when a tram she was travelling on overturned on the common above Argoed. She had been to Tredegar this day and was returning to Argoed. At the inquest, held at the Rock Inn, it was stated that the tyre of the tender wheel had come off and the train was thrown down the embankment. The last tram fell upon Abraham Richards and Mary Lloyd; she was later found dead under the tram. Robert Jones (Smith) to the Tredegar Company, reported that he had put on the tyre within a fortnight, and that it was properly put on. William Meredith proved that the road was in good condition and that he had examined it a quarter of an hour before the accident had occurred. Incidentally, the Meredith family had been connected with the maintenance of the tramroad since its inception in 1800—William Lewis Meredith, his father and grandfather were the company's Permanent Way Inspectors.

THE MEREDITH FAMILY

The above named was the last of the Meredith family to work on the maintenance of the Permanent Way of the Sirhowy Line. He was born in 1843 and died in 1924. His father, William Meredith, born in 1809 and died in 1886. The third was William Lewis ap Meredydd, born in 1760, and died in 1836. He was responsible for much of the original tramway construction from Sirhowy to Nine Mile Point. Both William Lewis Meredith and his father were born in Argoed. The paternal ancestors were descended from Lewellyn, the third son of Gwilym ap Philip of Rhiwbina, by Cardiff, who settled at Gwrhay, in the parish of Mynyddislwyn, circa 1425.

There were some strange local happenings years ago. Rhoswen Farm is on the left hand side of the road on the main road from Manmoel Crossing on the main road to Bedwellty. In the 1860s a gentleman farmer and local magistrate lived there—a man known as Matthew Ion. He took part in the social life of the village, chairing local concerts and meetings in places like the old Argoed Arms and Cwrt-y-bela School. He was a stickler for the law and had a boy working for him, named John Hexhy. The boy got fed up with the job and left without warning, but he was later brought before the court which consisted of local J.Ps. The court, under the Bedwellty Petty Sessional Division, was held at the Rock Inn before the Rev. Edmund Leigh, Rector of Bedwellty and Captain Marsh of Blackwood, a colliery proprietor. The boy was ordered to pay costs and return to work. That is how it was at that time, but it would be interesting to know how many hours the boy worked, and what cash, if any, he got for it. Mr. Ion did most of his travelling on horseback, and on one occasion met with a serious accident returning from Tredegar. The horse tripped on the bad roads and fell on him, causing severe bruising and a broken leg. He was returning from a Board of Guardians meeting at Tredegar on 27th May, 1865.

Mr. Ion owned three white race horses—Faith, Hope and Charity, and they raced at the Bedwellty three-mile Race Track in 1872, and were later buried in Berllanlwyd fields. They apparently had rare speed and jumping abilities.

Fire at Sunny View

In July 1926, London House was up for sale. It was situated on the corner of the main road and the village road at Sunny View, and in the V-section of ground to the south of the Primitive Methodist Chapel. Underneath, fronting on to the Argoed Village road, were two lock-up shops—the Co-op had them for some years. Isaiah Jenkins and his family were living there until the 1920s and the terrific fire which gutted the building and lower road shops. Only the small section near the chapel remained. It was a night I shall never forget! We were within yards of the inferno, and with a north-east wind going, we got the full force of it, with showers of sparks coming over the house. Mr. Jenkins was attending a Prayer Meeting at the Baptist Chapel when he was called for. It was said at the time that firemen trying to connect hoses to the hydrants on the main road and at Sunny View found them completely rusted up and unusable. The fire had been raging for about an hour before a water tender arrived—too late, except to dampen it down.

It was rebuilt a few years later. There was an ambulance box at the corner of the approach road down to the village. After the sale the premises were taken down and road improvements made.

Train Services

Passenger trains started running between Sirhowy and Newport on 19th June, 1865 and, as no transport existed of any consequence, business people, local doctors, chemists, etc., made use of the train guard, John Saunders, to bring urgent items for them from Newport—all unofficial, of course, but it worked extremely well. (It was the only way to get items quickly in those days). My father could just remember John Saunders when he came down the Valley to work in 1888 and recalls that John had a habit of talking to himself; his various clients, chiefly from Tredegar and Black-wood, would give him the money on the way down to Newport and usually the change left over was his. Sometimes he would be heard to exclaim 'not much over', with a few pertinent remarks to fit the occasion!

In the Argoed of eighty years ago rail was the only effective means of transport, and little was known of the happenings of the surrounding area, except by reading the local newspaper and Sundays were extremely quiet days.

Local Characters

I well remember Joseph Pope, school attendance officer, (Joe Pope, the 'Whipper-in') who used to scare the living daylights out of mothers and children alike when a visit was necessary. Mr. Pope started as a school attendance officer at Cwrt-y-bela School in January 1904. Fred Giles of Sunny View, Boot & Shoe Repairer, mouth filled with tacks and pulled them out one by one when hammering on a sole!

Local characters, like Fred, were to be found in every village, and Argoed was no exception. Tom Williams, born in the 1850s, was a local builder at Argoed and in the early days he was a part-time constable. Many tricks were played on him from time to time, but he was an excellent mason when the urge came on. One of his major undertakings was the retaining wall, now demolished, opposite the Rock Inn. The date 1897 was clearly cut into the coping stone on the Argoed end of the wall. During his constabulary duties he would proceed post-haste to the Bedwellty area if a disturbance was reported in the Cwm, which, I believe was fairly frequent in those days!

Tom Williams's father was also a builder and was working on the roof of a house in Bedwellty Village in 1839 when a contingent of Chartists passed by on their way from Tredegar to Blackwood, and in doing so removed the ladder, leaving his father up on the roof until assistance came! A favourite trick of the Williams' was the fitting of an electric shocking coil to the door on the inside at Christmas time—if the Carol Singers touched it—they made a hasty retreat! (It was, however, operated by batteries and not strong enough to do any harm). Tom's brother, Edmund, must surely be one of the first in Argoed to possess a motor licence. The Williams' were also the first to have electric light in Argoed when Edmund constructed a 500 watt dynamo from drawings in a contemporary engineering journal of 1909. The house wiring was good enough to take power, later when electric light came to the Argoed district.

Argoed's Resident Doctor

Argoed's first resident doctor was, of course, Dr. John Richard Griffiths, who had the house and surgery named 'Llwynfedw' built at the lower end of Gelynos Hill, but before this he lived at Sunny View. He was known locally by many as 'Dr. John' and did his round of visiting on a small two-stroke motor cycle; and by the expression on his face he always seemed to be assisting the engine in doing its job! In the days before the National Health Service most patients paid for their medical treatment quarterly, and if you made a personal visit, you received a glass of sherry on settling your bill. He and Mrs. Griffiths would occasionally take a first class ride on the train to Newport. He did not mix much with his patients. Sometimes he hosted a house party with his friend, the Vicar of Cwrt-y-bela Church, and I have it on good authority that a touch of Johnny Walker kept the conversation going and the Rev. Rees, on his way home, was helped through the Cwm by fireworks on one occasion!

My funniest recollection of the doctor was an incident which happened in Sunny View in the early 1930s when Gomer Thomas was delivering bread on his way up Sunny View. Suddenly the back door of his van sprang open, scattering loaves in all directions. Who should be coming up the hill behind him but Dr. John! It was a case of avoiding the onslaught of the loaves and the doctor did a series of zigzag turns worthy of any competitor in the Brands Hatch Motor Cycle Trials. In later years Dr. Cotton gave assistance to the doctor. Others were to follow including Dr. O'Rheidon and Dr. Reynolds and the partnership of Doctors Jones and Davies.

I recall Mr. Hough, headmaster of Argoed School, who lived at Blackwood and came up to the school on the morning train. He dressed like a gentleman farmer—I remember his leggings and heavy brown shoes, beautifully polished, and his bowler hat. Mr. Hough was secretary of the Bedwellty Show for many years.

Some of the older generation will remember John Morgan, the tea man; he came from Rhiw and Friday was his day for Argoed. When the conversation was over his final words were always 'Well, Dydd da a dioloh nawr' (Well, Good Day and thank you now) and away he would go, with his walking stick over his shoulder, and Gladstone-bag hooked on. He always wore dark clothes and a black soft trilby hat. His brother kept the Ironmonger's shop at Argoed.

With the closing of Pochin Colliery, the use of steam power ceased in the valley. I well remember a friend of mine taking me on a journey to see the North Winder at Oakdale Colliery. What an impressive piece of machinery it was, with its corris valve gear and a 'big end' worthy of the name. These fine engines were built by Markhams of Chesterfield, and were, without doubt, some of the finest ever made. I thought they combined beauty of line and symbol of power all in one.

The Horse and Cart

Up to 1925, and in many cases later, all the local hauling was done by horses—much of the household coal was brought around by Lewis Price of Pen-rhiw-eglwys Farm. More than once had I seen his horses on the ground coming up Sunny View in icy conditions, and it required experience and persuasion to bring them to their feet again. The fear of falling again seemed to affect them as much as it did us. Many other collieries delivered coal at that time, including Bowditch Bros Ltd., Christopher Pond of Blackwood; Budd & Co., of Rock Colliery, and of course, Abernant Colliery, of the Bargoed Coal Company. Coal was the major product and everyone had a coal fire. Other treacherous spots for the horses were at George Street, Woodville Terrace, Gelynos Avenue and the Cwm.

There were no bags then, the black diamond was tipped outside the house on the road, and it was up to the householder to get it in as best he or she could. For the colliers it was a tin bath in front of the kitchen fire, and often a long walk to and from work.

School Choir

Since the early 1920s Argoed School had quite a respectable choir, under its conductor, Evan Williams. The choir attended many Eisteddfodau and competed most years, visiting Abergavenny, Mountain Ash, and many times to the Central Hall at Newport.

I remember quite well the many arguments between Evan Williams and Gabriel Jenkins, our accompanist, and on one occasion it was over the song 'March, March, March, like Victors'. Unfortunately, we did not march like victors that day, but we came second out of seven choirs, and that was entirely due to singing it at the wrong time, a point Gabriel had insisted on all along, but Williams would not give in. The adjudicators remarks made it quite clear, we had the excellent tone and good balance and would have scored top marks, but sang it too slowly!

In practice, at school, Evan Williams came close to each singer in turn, and you offered up a little prayer that he caught you singing in tune!

We always travelled by train, and I can remember, in one instance, being pushed into the guard's van of a train at Nantybwch, presumably on our way to Abergavenny. I enjoyed every minute of it. Trains fascinated me from an early age, and I was always on the look-out for new engines or coaches or any new line-side features.

Transport

In 1921 Mr. John Watts, of Lydney purchased three army chassis, two of which were Albion chain-driven models, fitted with 26 seater bodies, and a third, a 32 seater Leyland Charabanc. This venture was given the title of 'The Valleys Motor Bus Services' and was put into service in the Tredegar—Ebbw Vale area in June 1921. The other routes were Tredegar—Brynmawr, via Ebbw Vale, and Tredegar to Pontllanfraith. A double-decker body was used on one of the models and I remember my father and I coming from Tredegar on one occasion on the open top deck, which had wooden slatted seats. It was a frightening experience for me and one needed a current insurance policy and a good nervous system as the road was only fit for horse-drawn traffic at the time. The service began at 11 a.m. and ran a two-hourly schedule until 9 p.m., and that was the first bus service to run through the Hollybush, Argoed and Blackwood area.

The return fare was expensive for the period, 3/2d (17p) return, Tredegar to Pontllanfraith. The Company became the Red & White Bus Company.

There were some buses in the Blackwood district before this. One of them, the Sirhowy Valley Motor Transport of Blackwood, was founded in 1919 and its secretary was Mr. R. T. Brown, who later became West Mon's Manager.

The Griffin acquired W. R. Evans of Blackwood and the Blackwood Motor Company in 1925—these were first in Blackwood, dating back to 1914. W. R. Evans was known as 'Billy Bun' and he made and sold buns as well as driving his bus!

When the Bedwellty U.D.C. made its first attempt to promote a Bill in 1926, they were strongly opposed by the local bus operators, especially

Lewis & James; but in the meantime the Mynyddislwyn U.D.C. promoted a similar Bill and eventually the two joined forces to form the West Monmouthshire Omnibus Board, who operated 17 vehicles at the time.

During 1929 Western Services made an arrangement with Lewis & James (later acquired by Western Welsh Co. Ltd.) for the operation of a pooled service between Tredegar and Newport. West Mon also ran a Blackwood—Manmoel service twice weekly, now operated by Glyn Evans with a mini-bus. Local transport for day trips with a Leyland Charabanc was provided by William Harris, of Gelynos Avenue, Argoed.

The railway passenger service between Nantybwch and Newport closed in June 1960—it commenced on 19th June, 1865. During the 'North Western's (L&NWR) reign, which ended in 1923, and for a few years later, trains were packed at weekends and at holiday times. There were many excursions to places in the north, including Blackpool, and the cities of Glasgow and Edinburgh.

Regular excursions in the summer to Barry Island continued for many years and in 1930 these were the fares:—

> Barry Island, return 3/9d
> Barry Island, half-day 2/6d
> Cardiff, half-day (for football matches) 1/6d

Temperance Societies, the Chapels, Clubs and Schools all made use of these trains. These excursions ran to Barry Island until 1959, just a year before the railway closed.

One of the longest passenger trains ever to run, was in September 1948, when a special took members of the Woodbine Workmens' Club, Blackwood and their wives, to Weston-super-Mare and Cheddar on their annual outing. The train consisted of seventeen coaches and two engines. Until 1924 the signalmen at Hollybush, Markham, Argoed and Blackwood rang the signal-box handbell to announce the approach of the passenger trains, although this ritual probably went on unnoticed by most passengers.

Evan Jones was the first Station Master at Argoed in 1866. In the 1920s Frank Reynolds was a clerk at Argoed before his appointment as station master—he started his railway service as a porter at Ebbw Vale. He was transferred to Abersychan and Talywain, from where he retired. At that time, Len Hurdle was the booking and invoicing clerk at Argoed. There was a small goods shed behind the up platform which was rented to Crawford's Biscuits; these biscuits were collected by motor van driven by Mr. Pewsey, who lived on the new road.

Argoed Baptist Chapel

The Baptist community at Argoed grew up around Mr. William Meredith who lived at Pwll-y-Pant alongside the Sirhowy Tramroad. In 1811 his home was duly licenced for the purposes of holding religious services until the Baptist Chapel was built in 1817. He and others were already members of Baptist Churches as in the case of Richard Lewis and his wife who were founders of Siloh Baptist Church, Tredegar. Also from Tredegar came James Howells and his wife, and William Rees and his son. From Blaina, Mr. and Mrs. David Richards; from Hengoed, William Davies; from Caerphilly, Lewis Jones and from Bethesda, David Lewis.

One of the principal benefactors was a Mr. Yorath, noted for his generosity. He placed his house at their disposal for the first Baptismal Service, which took place in 1811 and was conducted by the Rev. John Jenkins of Hengoed. Mr. Yorath also came to their aid by granting them land for a chapel and burial ground on a lease of 999 years at a nominal rental of 1/- per annum! He also provided all the stone required—yet he was not a member himself of the little Baptist Community!

The Chapel was completed by the end of July 1817, the first sermon being preached by the Rev. Harry Evan Harry, the son of Evan Harry, of Blaenau. Membership at the time was 37. The first Deacons were James Howells, Lewis James, and William Edmunds. Early in 1818, the Rev. Thomas Davies was invited to become a Pastor at Argoed; he was a native of Penyparc, near Cardigan and was a poet of no mean ability. His preaching, on one occasion, brought members of sixteen churches to Argoed on a Communion Sunday. He remained at Argoed until his death at 63 years of age. A tablet was placed behind the pulpit bearing the following:—

ER COF AM Y PARCH
Thomas Davies
Esgob Cyntaf Yr Eglwys hon
Yr hwn a fu farw Medi 4 ydd 1841
yn 63 Milwydd oed

The Rev. Thomas Evans of Llanrwst took over in October 1842 and after a ministry of five and a half years returned to Llanrwst in 1848. He was followed by the Rev. John Jarman from Victoria, Ebbw Vale. Although his pastorate was short, just a little over two years, another thirty-eight members were added to the church at Argoed. He resigned in May 1851 and went to Henllys, near Newport. By this time membership had risen to 136 and the Sunday School had an attendance of 125 children.

In 1851 it was decided to rebuild the Chapel and also extend the burial ground at a total cost of £400. There were then two 'short stay' Ministers, the Rev. Lewis James, a native of New Quay, when attendance fell to 59 and the Sunday School to 70 scholars, followed by the Rev. Thomas Griffiths, when membership made a dramatic recovery to 129, and the Sunday School to 123!

The Rev. W. T. Davies of Pontypool College came to Argoed in 1862, and he was followed by the Rev. William Thomas when it was decided to build a house for him in 1874.

The next Minister was the Rev. Evan George, also of Pontypool College—he married a niece of Mr. Isaac Jenkins, a faithful deacon of the Church. He brought his Ministry to a close in September 1900. During Mr. George's pastorate, the vestry was built at a cost of £300. The contractor was Mr. Thomas Jenkins of Argoed. The Church was again renovated in 1901, prior to this the Baptistry was situated outside the Chapel where the porch of the vestry now stands.

The Rev. David Morgan excepted the cordial invitation of the Church and commenced his Ministry on Sunday, 7th June, 1903, staying over nine and a half years. Known as 'Morgan Barry Dock', he proved himself very efficient, and had the privilege of receiving over 200 into the church membership, of which 146 were baptized. During his stay, a very successful Sunday School was opened at Cwm Corrwg. In 1913 he resigned his pastorship at Argoed to go to Calvary, Port Talbot, (the membership at Argoed when he left was 205). In the same year the Church was again renovated at a cost of £400; heating apparatus and gas having been installed. The Rev. J. Emlyn Jones's ordination took place in November 1915. The much respected Rev. John Jenkins of Argoed was among those taking part. The Baptists are still at Argoed, although considerably fewer in number, but doing well when compared with the Church of England at Cwrt-y-bela, where services ceased in 1969 when the church was demolished.

Quoting the 'Monmouthshire Merlin' for 27th July, 1867:—

> The choir of 40 strong were treated to a hot supper by the Rev. Rees Jones at his residence, Myrtle Grove, Blackwood. After supper, Mr. Jones presented Mr. Loftus Munroe with a beautiful silver mounted dressing case in acknowledgement of his kindness in presiding at the harmonium at the Church during the last six years'.

Looking back to the time when the Church was demolished and when the congregation dwindled to less than a dozen, it is hard to realise now that once there was a church choir of forty at Cwrt-y-bela.

The Methodists' membership at Argoed and the Rock, like so many other Welsh towns and villages, has dwindled over the years, relying on the faithful few for existence. Years ago, the Primitive Methodists at Argoed were in the Rhymney Valley circuit under the Rev. William Tootel.

Sport

Sport was very popular at Argoed in the early part of this century. There were football teams at Cwrt-y-bela and Gwrhay, and Argoed Ramblers played on the Ynys field near the river, a place from where the ball was often retrieved! Changing rooms were at the Argoed Arms Hotel. Cricket was also very popular, with first and second teams playing in a field near Bedwellty Church.

Argoed also, was the venue for International Quoits Matches and I remember Lord Raglan opening the ground behind the Argoed Arms Hotel. The Argoed Quoits Club was formed well over 100 years ago and Jack Price had the honour of winning the Welsh and Monmouthshire Championship on three occasions. Official scorers included well-known Argoed names, regrettably no longer with us, including Charlie Dodd, Dai Thomas, Morgan Lewis and Tom Jeanes.

The first ground was near the Castle Hotel in the Cwm, transferred afterwards to the rear of the Argoed Arms Hotel, but a new ground was opened later at the Colliers Arms, Gwrhay, only to be brought back finally to the back of the Argoed Arms, Argoed (see captions 97-100).

The Tennis Club was well established and had its Clubhouse down on the Ynys field. During construction, turf for the court was cut at Trefil and carted to Argoed by the founders of the club because of its quality.

There was also some entertainment and the occasional supper at the Ex-Servicemens Institute, Argoed. On one such occasion, in January 1926, there were over 50 present, the MCs being Leslie Dodd and I. M. Davies. Among those present were Mr. James Panes, Miss Nancy Morgan, D. Panes, W. Dodd, A. W. Jones, W. Harler, S. Lewis, H. Morgan, C. Parsons, Maud John and many others. When the football matches were over and the pubs turned out on a Saturday night, they would all congregate on the Cwm Bridge for a sing song, which could be heared all over Argoed.

Cwm Crach Colliery, Argoed

There must still be some people alive today who remember the Cwm Crach Colliery Incline. The trams ran down from the Level near the top of Sunny View under the main road to the side of the railway, where the screens were situated for tipping the coal into wagons.

Although the colliery was opened very early in the nineteenth century under various names—Cwm Crach, Argoed Level, etc., it is difficult to pinpoint the actual date of the Incline. From old maps, it seems, at one time the coal was transferred to wagons in front of the old cottages near the Baptist Chapel and hauled up through the village by horses to the station yard. Later, a connection was made with the main line at the lower end of the village where the screens were situated last before the closure.

By 1900, and probably before, the trams were running down the Incline, and across the village road from Sunny View, to the screens on the railway side—I remember them crossing the steep hill to the village until approximately 1922, when the colliery closed. The Incline was worked on the balance principle, the full trams going down bringing the 'empties' up. At the top was a Band Brake, the control lever of which was worked by Old Jim who came up from Pontllanfraith each day on the 8.30 a.m. morning train; I never knew his real name. There was a small cabin at the top of the

Incline where Jim had his midday meal, and was often engaged in conversation with a fellow traveller on the morning train—Mr. Hough, the Argoed Schoolmaster.

Like Rock, there were two headings at Cwm Crach, the original one going up on the east side of the dingle, the trams crossing over the Nant Crach (Crack Brook) on their way out, and the second heading bearing sharp left under the Bedwellty road, (this one was in use last before the colliery closed); near the first heading was a small Blacksmith's Shop. The smith, in the 1910-20 period, being one of the Bunston family. During the 1920s the Bedwellty road subsided several times near the Level mouth, and the watchman was Mr. Jeanes (father of the late Tom Jeanes) who had a small sentry box and a roaring fire going in the brazier at the side of the road. He was there when darkness fell, and through the night, and occasionally burst into Salvation Army hymn tunes! In those days children gathered around late into the evening.

Prior to this, Mr. Jeanes provided the Argoed area with a valuable service—that of bread making. To do this he walked over Penyfan to Webb's Brewery at Aberbeeg to purchase balm. This was a by-product in the process of brewing, and he carried it over in two large jacks to sell at ½d per cup for drinking and 3d per basin for bread-making.

The Ground Frame, Protection Signal and Colliery siding for Cwm Crach Colliery was taken out about 1924. In the old days there were a small number of Coke Ovens at the bottom of the Incline, near the cottages in front of the Chapel. These and the Chapel were later rebuilt. Tramps frequented the old coke ovens at night to get warmth and rest. The area was covered with slag heaps and refuse from the level. The Sunny View tip was one such slag heap, but was there long before the houses.

The tip was cut down and landscaped in 1950 by contractors from Birmingham and in shot firing, they damaged the house near the Incline, occupied at that time by Mr. and Mrs. Evans, and also to houses at the top of Sunny View. The residents of Sunny View saw the full effect of daylight for the first time! All Sunny View children played on the tip at one time or another, and I remember one old resident, Chas Jones, saying to me on one occasion, 'Well, what a glorious view'—it was a clear day, and the scene was magnificent.

I went up there to watch the trains! On a Saturday morning, in the summer, as many as five excursion trains would run to Barry Island, and this was an excellent spot to see them from. The view was clear from the Common, above Argoed Station, to the Parson's Bridge below Fairoak. In the still of the night one could hear the church bells from Bedwellty and, with the wind in the right direction, the clock bell on the old coachhouse at Maesrudded.

There were no females employed at Cwm Crach Colliery. During 1840, the proprietors were the Tredegar Colliery Company, who employed about eighty adults, forty-one youths under eighteen, and twenty under thirteen years old were also working there at this time—some of these were six years or even younger!

It was the custom at that time to pay the colliers in public houses, but those at Cwm Crach were always paid in the office, and the company did not have their own shop. The men were on strike for fourteen weeks in 1840, and work was often irregular. Some men depended on begging at the Tredegar Iron Works, but they helped one another in extreme cases. Colliers were earning 12/- a week and boys varied from 6d to 2/6d a day according to age and job. Domestic coal was 6/6d for 21 cwt, and small coal (slack) 1/- for 10 cwt.

The Colliery had many proprietors over the years. They included:—

Lewis and John Jenkins.
E. D. Williams.
Tredegar Colliery Co.—1840.
Slater & Baker, Bristol.
Happerfield & Williams, Newport.
Melvin Lloyd, Castleton, Cardiff.
James Richards & Co., Bute Docks, Cardiff.
Budd & Co., (who, I believe, were the last to work the colliery).

At the Rhoswen Colliery of Bevan & Pryce a new incline was made from the Colliery to screens alongside the Sirhowy Railway, and in 1874 Gwillim Jenkins built the incline wall, and started work on the Coke Ovens. When the new road from Tredegar to Argoed was made during 1893-4 bridges were required over the inclines at Rhoswen and Cwm Crach Collieries; traces of these can still be seen.

Geology

There are widespread deposits of boulder clay in the northern part of the Sirhowy Valley around Argoed and small areas of sand and gravel occur at Gwrhay. About a mile south of Gwrhay, gravel lies in the valley floor and forms an unbroken deposit as far as Gelligroes. The sandstone is exposed in Nant Cwm-Crach (near the Argoed Farm, Argoed Urchf) overlaying some thirty to forty feet of mudstone, siltstone and thin sandstone forming the upper part of the sequence between it and the Mynyddislwyn area.

The pennant rock meausres are believed to attain a maximum thickness in the Blackwood area near to the old Libanus Pit of 450 feet and due to this, it was possible to walk for miles through the workings without fear of a roof fall. You could enter, for instance, at the Rock Level, near the river, and come out at Pond's Primrose Colliery at the Rock.

At the Rock Colliery, (known later as Budds Rock Colliery), near the St. Margaret's Church, coal was brought to the surface from many workings in the area. The original heading was situated between the railway and the river, behind Rock House, and was opened about 1825. Many men were killed by roof falls here, and in one instance, on 14th September, 1855, Edwin Roberts was drowned by an eruption of water, caused probably by breaking into old workings. Henry Marsh was the owner at this time. The Shaft and Wooden Headgear near the church was sunk and built after 1885 and was used for bringing coal only to the surface.

Llanover Colliery

Llanover Colliery was sunk about 1912 to the Brithdir seam. The name comes from the Llanover Estate and Lady Llanover. During sinking operations on Easter Sunday, two men were killed when the cage they were in plummetted to the pit bottom. It seems the mechanism preventing the cage overriding the Pit Headgear had stuck, and in trying to reverse the procedure, the rope broke. In the construction of the colliery, little was used in new material in order to cut down the cost. The colliery's manager, Mr. O'Connor saw to that, and used scrap iron in large quantities and metalwork from the Shipbreakers Yard. Mr. Edgar Paine of Argoed, commenced work at Llanover at thirteen years of age—they were ten hour shifts then, and the weekly wage was 10/6d (52.5p)!

In an emergency there was access to Abernant Colliery, and also to a level at Hollybush.

Llanover played a major part in preventing flood water reaching Oakdale Colliery. The plant consisted of two Hathorn Davey Steam Pumps installed about 1910-12, and due to the pumps being overloaded, water rose at times to 80 feet in the shaft. The Bargoed Company obtained the services of a diver for maintenance of the pumps at pit bottom. Mr. H. J. Rake provided a very ingenious method to supply the diver with air while he was working on the small single cage platform. In March 1931, a 60,000 gallons per hour Sulzer Sinking Pump was installed; the electricity coming from overhead lines passing nearby. Later, Llanover was taken over by the Tredegar Iron & Coal Company, and two Deepwell Electric Pumps were suspended into the shaft. The pumps' bearings were lined with Lignum Vitae, and lubricated with filtered water. During the 1920s I remember the Colliery as a very untidy looking place with old pipes, angle iron and corrugated sheets strewn all over the place.

Abernant Colliery

Abernant Colliery was situated near one of the valley's beauty spots, Pont Abernant-y-felin, where the road from Bedwellty to Manmoel crossed the Sirhowy River by a picturesque bridge. Alas, it is no longer there. A concrete structure has replaced it.

Towards the end of 1888 sinking operations began at Abernant and the black diamond was first struck on Thursday morning, 20th March, 1890.

The seam was 3 feet thick. On the 3rd May, 1890 all men employed by the Company were given a dinner and plenty of brown ale in celebration at Church House, Bedwellty. The catering was done by Richard Evans of the Argoed Arms and Mr. T. Saunders of the Church Inn, Bedwellty. Mr. Kirke of Llanishen, Cardiff and Mr. J. J. Williams, two of the directors, joined in the festivities. Also present was Mr. Morgan Thomas, the engineer. In 1888, there was no road to Abernant from Argoed or the Tredegar direction, but colliers' trains were soon running in both directions and platforms were set up on each side of the line near the colliery.

Abernant produced some of the finest smith coal in South Wales. To introduce it to prospective customers, 1,000 sample bags of coal were made up and despatched in 1890, each to a different consignee.

The first stack of buff bricks was built in 1888. The second stack of red bricks was demolished on 19th July, 1936. These bricks were put to good use for some were purchased by Mr. Edwards, who built the bungalow at Sunny View, Argoed on what was formerly London Midland & Scottish Railway Land. Mr. Edwards also used material from the old Cwrt-y-bela School; and so Argoed still maintains a material link with the past. The Colliery closed between 1932 and 1933; the shaft was 480 feet deep to the Brithdir seam. The Managers were Mr. Edwin Rosser, followed by Mr. William O'Connor and Mr. Williams. The Company's Offices were at 50 George Street, Docks Cardiff. In 1916, 418 worked underground and 59 on top.

An incident which occurred at the Colliery in September 1909 could have proved disastrous were it not for the keen observation of Mr. Harrow, the winder. As he was lowering the men down the shaft he discovered the bedding of the engine had given away; he slowed down at once and fortunately no accident occurred. The men had to return to the surface through the air pit by means of a bowk. As the cage capacity was limited to about five men, it was some considerable time before all the colliers were brought to the surface. It was possible later to gain exit at Hollybush.

Manmoel Village

To reach Manmoel Village we re-cross the river, and turn sharp right, getting to Pont Abernant-y-felin and on to the zig-zag road to Manmoel Village. In dry weather you can also take a very pleasant walk up through the dingle. Its church, the Paran Presbyterian, celebrated one hundred and fifty years in 1978. This little church with a seating capacity of just 100 was built in 1828 to serve the farming community, but before this, services were held in the farmhouses with some worshippers coming on horseback. Today they come by car and minibus.

It is believed the movement at Manmoel dates back to the time when Hywel Harris toured the Argoed area preaching the Gospel. Later, towards the end of the eighteenth century David Wynne and his family came from Eglwysbach, near Llangeitho, and established the church at Manmoel. Incidentally, Hywel Harris received a threatening letter from John Perrott who was, at that time, curate at Mynyddislwyn Church; Harris had preached in the churchyard without Perrott's permission.

The Perrotts came from Hay-on-Wye in Breconshire to Bedwellty in the 17th century. Their three sons were Gregory and Walter who settled at Bedwellty, and John who made his home at Trevethin. John Perrot graduated at New Inn Hall, Oxford in December 1725 and became Rector of Gelligaer in 1729. Manmoel School was built in 1880 when the Mistress at that time was Miss Hussey.

The Bedwellty Area

The Parish Church at Bedwellty is one of the oldest and most striking landmarks in Monmouthshire. The name is involved in much obscurity. Situated about 1,000 feet above sea level, it is dedicated to Saint Sannan, an Irish Saint.

Controversy exists about the origin and meaning of the name 'Bedwellty'. There was an abundance of birch trees in the vicinity, so we have 'Bedw-elltyd'—birch groves. Another explanation, although highly improbable, is the name Bedd-tyn-Wyllt, 'the wild man's grave'. The Rev. William Fothergill, writing in the booklet 'The Legend of Bedwellty' observed Byd-gwell-ty or Byd-well-iti which, translated means 'A better world to thee'. Another writer suggests Bodwellte, 'The House of Wellte'. Most of the 'Bod' place names are associated with persons, generally Saints. A map, dated 1610, shows the spelling as Bydwelthye.

With a genuine beacon tower, ideally situated, signals could be transmitted from Bedwellty to the Brecon Beacons and Caerphilly Castle, and also to the churches of Mynyddislwyn and Gelligaer, although the slag heaps in the Rhymney Valley now affect the visibility of the latter.

Many years ago, the church formed a part of the monasterial domain of Glastonbury with Bassaleg. It was, however, separated from Glastonbury, by one of the Abbots and handed as a gift to the See of Llandaff.

The church at Bedwellty and Bassaleg have the same structural features—squat square towers and double-sloped parallel roofs, which suggests a common designer or builder. An interesting relic is the Priests' Door, circa 1220, which opens into the chancel on the south side. It is made of oak, and studded with iron bolts, giving an appearance of immense strength, and shows how carefully guarded the churches were in times of turmoil and disturbances years ago.

The church registers date back to 1624 and then to 1732, the entries are made in Latin and are beautifully written on Vellum. From the latter date they are entered in English, with a variety of styles of handwriting. In the chancel can be found one of the finest vestment chests in South Wales, dating from approximately 1450. Considering the age of this chest, the carvings are in a remarkably good state of preservation. Sundials are frequently found in early churchyards, and occasionally on church towers as at Mathern; unfortunately all that remains of the one at Bedwellty is the base and rugged stone pillar.

The original ring of six bells were cast by the famous firm of John Taylor & Sons, Loughborough in 1895 and two more by the same firm in 1920. They bear the following interesting inscriptions:—

1. To the Glory of God.   25"
   Given by C. Pond, in loving memory of wife, Mrs. A. J. Pond, 1920.
2. On Earth Peace.   26"
   R. Roberts,   Rector.
   C. Pond.
   E. Edwards.   1920.
   P. L. Lloyd.
3. Sarah Strelley of Oakerthorpe, Derbyshire, 1895.   30"
4. In memory of the Blessed.   30"
5. In memory of Rees and Emily Lewis.   33"
6. Emily, wife of Rees Lewis, of Dryssiod, Ebbw Vale.
   Died February 1st 1895, 58 years.   34¼"
7. Rees Lewis Esq., of Dryssiod, Ebbw Vale, departed this Life, March 22nd 1889.   63 years.   38"
8. This peal of six bells was given to this Church of Bedwellty Sarah Gertrude, wife of Richard Charles Strelley Esq., in loving memory of her father and mother, Rees and Emily Lewis.   1895.   42½"

Before the ring of six bells erected in 1895, and increased to eight in 1920, there was a bell dated 1815, known as the 'Waterloo Bell', forming one of a collection of six bells in the possession of Mr. Edmund Jones of Fforest, Pontneddfechan, Glam.

The Waterloo Bell was cast by Jasper Westcott & Sons, Bristol and eventually went to St. Edmunds Church, Roath, Cardiff.

All the inscriptions are on the bell waist.

Christopher Pond was the proprietor of several collieries, including the Primrose Colliery at the Rock; while the Rev. R. W. Roberts was a very popular Rector at Bedwellty at this time. Edward Edwards, of Maesygarn was a one time Manager of the Maesrudded Estate, shown on ordnance survey map as 'Maes-rhyddid', and P. L. Lloyd (Phil) the Landlord of the Argoed Arms Hotel.

The Church was without a lectern until the late J. G. James, J.P., of Tynewydd, presented a beautiful one in the form of a brass eagle, in memory of his father and mother. A recent inspection in 1985 revealed that the church tower and bells needed major renovation work, and a restoration fund was set up by the congregation, which raised upward of £20,000 towards the approximate figure of £45,000 needed.

Early Incumbents of Bedwellty

1815—John Edwards	1859—Rees Hubert Morgan
1840—William Leigh Morgan	1870—Edward Jones
1844—William Jones	1872—Samuel John
1846—Edmund Leigh	1893—Richard Jones

The organ was presented in 1900 by Evan Thomas of Builth, in memory of his wife, Rachel Thomas. This instrument was completely overhauled a few years ago at considerable expense and is still in use.

The organist at Bedwellty for many years was Mr. Kilbourn, who got £16 a year for his duties. The organ blower (they were hand blown in those days) got the princely sum of £1.5.0d (£1.25p) a year! Mr. Cliff Mantle followed Mr. Kilbourn as organist.

The year 1638 recorded the visitation of a plague which carried off 109 victims (some records say 82). Tradition has it that everyone, except three living in the Parish were tragic victims.

The following are extracts from a booklet entitled 'The Legend of Bedwellty' by the Rev. William Fothergill, Assistant Curate of St. Mary Magdalene's, Munster Square, London—1859. The Fothergills were a Westmorland family and the first Richard Fothergill had brothers John and William; the latter became a curate in London. The family were involved in the early development of the Sirhowy and Tredegar Ironworks:—

> 'The Valley called the "Birchen World". Here stands the ancient remains of what was evidently once a noble house—aged people living thereabouts say these ruins have always been the same, and that their fathers never knew them different. They mark the spot where the last man lived—the last man in the Parish before ever the Parish was known as Bedwellty Parish. His name was Gomer ap Llyder'.

The Rev. Edmund Leigh, Incumbent of Bedwellty, 1846-59, wrote the following letter to the Rev. Fothergill in May 1859, his last year in office:—

> Bedwellty Parsonage
> May 13 1859
>
> Dear Sir,
> There is an aged woman in this Parish called 'Mary Gwaun-y-borfa' who informs me that she has got it from her grandfather, how that a plague so depopulated the parish as to leave none eventually to bury the dead. And in the manner in which those who died of the plague (owing to the frequency of deaths), were buried by laying them on the floor of the Church, and then heaping mould on them.
>
> The fact of the base of the pillars being buried fifteen inches is here accounted for; and the additional fact of an extraordinary quantity of human bones being found at that depth, when the church, undergoing restoration, was excavated to its proper level, seems to me strongly to corroborate the tradition respecting the plague, and the mode in

which they who died of it had been disposed of. There were cartloads of skeletons found so near the surface that I cannot account for their presence there on any other grounds than of the tradition.

You may make what use shall suit you of this, and believe me to be,
My dear Sir,   Yours faithfully,
Edmund Leigh

Rev. W. Fothergill.

Mary Gwaun-y-borfa's information obviously refers to the 1638 outbreak.

The source of Nant Crach is within yards of Saint Sannan's Well (Ffynnon Sant Sannan) close to Perry's Cottage and within sight of the Parish Church. Centuries ago, these Holy Wells were celebrated for their supposed medicinal virtues, although some sources indicate that the well water may have been responsible for the plague. (Paratyphoid).

Near to Perry's Cottage, on the other side of the road, is the Rectory, built in 1856; before this the clergy lived at Myrtle Grove, Blackwood.

The church was floodlit on Wednesday, 12th May, 1937, Coronation Day.

The Williams Family,
Maesruddud (the Meadow of Freedom)

Early history records that there was a settlement here in the 15th century or earlier. The present house was built for E. D. Williams about 1890 on early foundations. The driveway, gates and lodges were built in 1912, and there was an extensive library. The Coachouse and Clock turret are still there. Edmund Davies Williams was the second son of Edmund Williams, J.P., and succeeded his eldest brother, William Williams, who was known locally as 'Squire Williams'. There were two sisters, Mary and Margaret Williams. Mary Williams married T. Llewelyn Brewer in 1864; Margaret remained a spinster and lived with her brother at Maesruddud.

Miss Mary Williams married T. Llewellyn Brewer, of Danygraig, Christchurch, Newport at Bedwellty Church in February 1864. Flags and bunting spanned the road from Maesruddud to the Church, and cannons roared in the vicinity of Argoed. When the wedding party arrived, the church was crowded and hundreds of people could not gain admission. So great was the crush that, in spite of the existence of the two excellent Church Wardens, Mr. Howells of Gwalod-y-wain and Mr. Davies of Neuadd-wen, 'considerable difficulty was met with in keeping order'. The marriage was solemnised by the Rev. T. M. Davies, cousin of the bride.

A report of the marriage appeared in the 'Monmouthshire Merlin' of February 1864.

E. D. Williams died intestate on 21st January, 1895 and was buried in the family vault at Bedwellty. He was born at Maesruddud on 4th May, 1828, and over the years was a Justice of the Peace and Deputy Lieutenant of the County. He was High Sheriff of Monmouthshire in the Queen's Jubilee Year of 1887.

Although the funeral was private, many of his personal friends, and a large number of the inhabitants of the district, assembled to meet the funeral cortège at the church, where his ancestors had been interred in the family vault for generations.

At the Church, after lessons, the hymn 'O God our Help in Ages Past' was sung, and at the grave side the well-known Welsh Hymn 'Bydd Myrdd o Ryfeddodau'.

Mr. Williams had been Captain of the local Artillery Volunteers at Blackwood and his remains were interred with full military honours. He was not married, and the next male heir to the property was his nephew, Mr. E. T. Llewellyn Brewer, M.A. (St. Johns College, Oxford) and J.P. for the County of Monmouth. Captain Williams was Governor of Lewis School, Pengam, and was also well known to the children of the district, and to the Hollybush Schoolroom in particular. He was instrumental in the building of the Drill Hall at Blackwood. The local papers portrayed him as a true Christian and genuine friend. Mr. Williams was Chairman of the bench in the Tredegar Police Division and a faithful administrator of the law. He left £62,622.18.2p and the estate covered 464 acres.

On 15th June, 1895, Letters of Administration to the estate of E. D. Williams were granted out of the principal Registry to Margaret Williams, spinster, and Mary Brewer, widow, 'the natural and lawful sister and only next of kin'; but on 20th January, 1913, Mary Brewer died intestate and her son, E. T. Llewellyn Brewer-Williams, who was born on 6th September, 1865 took the name of Williams under Royal Licence and became heir-at-law to Edmund Davies Williams. By this time, Margaret Williams had also died.

The son married a native of the London area and lived at Maesruddud for a time. The family travelled frequently to London, and before the advent of the car, would take the horse-drawn carriage to Blackwood station and a first class ticket on the train. The family house of the Brewer's was at Danygraig, Christchurch, Newport.

Markham Village

Newspapers of the day described Markham as a Garden Village—near Argoed founded by the Markham Steam Coal Company. It was stated that a site of about forty acres had been purchased midway between Argoed and Hollybush for the erection of about 400 houses by the Markham Steam Coal Company, the building commenced in 1913.

The village and colliery takes its name after Sir Arthur Markham, a director of the Tredegar Iron & Coal Company, and the cost of the scheme was estimated to be approximately £100,000. The colliery was the first in the Sirhowy Valley to have electric winding gear. Building materials for the village came to a siding on the railway and were hauled up on inclines to different parts as the work progressed; the Hollybush end was completed first, the Abernant Road much later.

Mr. Lewis was the first station master when the station opened in 1917 and Mr. Thomas Foulkes was in charge of the Post Office in the 1920s. Markham School was opened in 1927.

An explosion occurred at the Markham Colliery on Saturday, 18th May before sinking operations had been completed. Five men were killed and many more injured on this occasion.

The following is an extract which appeared in a contemporary newspaper:

> 'The Markham Pit in the Sirhowy Valley where the explosion occurred on Saturday resulted in five deaths. It was stated on good authority that Sir Arthur Markham, with the Manager of the Colliery, and two sinkers went down and inspected the wreckage of the lodge-room, which had not been previously visited, and what may prove to be the probable cause of the explosion was found on the floor in the shape of a spent match.

> ### THE INQUEST.

> The Inquest was opened at Tredegar Police Court yesterday by Mr. Walford, the District Coronor. The jury composed of residents of Tredegar, who had previously visited the scene of the disaster.

> It must be gratifying to them at Tredegar to know that this was the first occasion in the history of the country where a life was saved by means of the rescue apparatus. Several men were injured.'

The Manager at the time was Mr. W. D. Wooley.

Mr. Cyril Davies, of Markham, is the proud possessor of a watch presented to his grandfather, James Davies, who was one of the first to enter the shaft after the explosion. It is suitably inscribed as follows:—

> 'Presented to James Davies by the Directors of Markham Steam Coal Company for heroism at the Markham Explosion, May 18th 1912'.

The Markham & District Colliery Band gave a Golden Jubilee concert at the Miners' Welfare Institute, Blackwood on Saturday, 16th September, 1978 to celebrate its formation 50 years ago. The following information on the history of the Band has been kindly supplied by the then Chairman, Mr. W. R. Hamer:—

> 'The Band was formed in 1928 and was known as the Markham British Legion Band, its first rehearsal room being a shed at the back of a cafe in Markham. In 1930 the Band became the Markham and District Colliery Silver Prize Band. As membership grew it became necessary to obtain extra instruments and with a loan from the local Miners Welfare Institute a complete set of new instruments was pur-

chased in 1932. It was about this time that a very active ladies committee was formed and they soon set about organising carnivals and comic football matches. The Band's first set of uniforms was purchased with money raised at these functions and was worn for the first time at a Marching and Deportment Contest at Fairford, Gloucester. This contest became an annual event for the Band and along with appearances at the famous Crystal Place remains a highlight of the Band's pre-war activities.

After the war the Band went through difficult times, struggling to restore its membership to the pre-war level. Fortunately, through the efforts of a small group of dedicated bandsmen, a Junior Band was formed in the village and the Senior Band was soon to reap the benefits of this new venture. The enthusiasm of the young players was such that they not only attended the twice weekly rehearsals for the Junior Band but also attended the "Big Band" rehearsals three times a week. This surely laid the foundations on which the Band's success in later years was built. The long ascent to Championship Standard had begun and was eventually achieved in 1958.

In 1968 the Band became Champion Band of Wales and as such were the only civilian band to play at the Investiture of H.R.H. Prince of Wales at Caernarvon Castle in 1969. Between 1969 and 1976 the Band has been one of the two bands chosen to form the National Brass Band of Wales performing at the National Eisteddfod throughout Wales and also at the Royal Albert Hall in 1976 when they took part in the Fifth Festival of 1,000 Welsh Male Voices. This concert was recorded by B.B.C. Television and has been released as a record.

Over the years the Band has won First Prizes at the National Eisteddfod Newtown, Ruthin and Criccieth and numerous other competitions, its most recent success being at the C.I.S.W.O. Contest at Trecynon in June of this year when it won first prize and qualified to compete at the Coal Board National Finals at Blackpool in November.

I have deliberately left one of the Band's finest achievements until last. In 1967 the Band moved into its very own Band Room which was purchased and eventually paid for out of contributions and prize monies won by the Band. This move was, without doubt, one of the major contributory factors which helped to establish Markham Band as one of the best in the Country. The number of appearances in the National Finals of Great Britain at the Royal Albert Hall and Coal Board Finals in recent years support this claim.

The luxury of having its own Band Room was short lived because on 2nd January 1976, the Band Room, along with many valuable instruments, music, uniforms and record books was destroyed in a freak storm. Unfortunately the Band was not insured against storm and tempest and therefore, found themselves in a very similar situation as the founder members faced fifty years ago. The long haul back has started with the formation of a Junior Band at Blackwood Comprehensive School—where any youngsters wishing to take up Brass Bands as a hobby will be more than welcome—and also the reformation of the ladies committee. The ladies have already held several Jumble Sales in the locality and plan to hold more in the near future. Despite the strenuous efforts of our President, Mr. Neil Kinnock, M.P., and the Band Committee, they have been unable to obtain financial support to rebuild the Band Room and once again find themselves dependent on the generosity of local organisations to provide rehearsal facilities. We hope this situation will not last too long and are looking for some kind of sponsorship which will help us to continue making music, not only for ourselves but for the pleasure of others.'

W. Hamer, Chairman

Under its present Conductor, Mr. D. V. Hendy, the band is very much back on form, winning many 'firsts' in various parts of the country.

Hollybush

On the 1858-60 map for the conversion of Sirhowy Tramroad to a railway, little is indicated of the Hollybush area; in fact, there are only three landmarks shown—the Ancient Druid Beer House, the Hollybush Inn and Hollybush Pit. It was not until 1868, when E. D. Williams bought the Hollybush Colliery, that any building of note appeared.

Gwillim Jenkins of Argoed built six houses and a schoolroom in 1874 for E. D. Williams. At this time the railway was single and the Hollybush station had just one platform, situated on the up side of the line, higher up the valley above the Colliery. The station, complete with Station Masters House, as we knew it last, was built in 1891 when double track was laid between Tredegar and Pontllanfraith. There was a time when flower beds and hanging baskets were to be seen on the platforms. The renovated station house is one of the few railway buildings still standing today in the Sirhowy Valley. The Turnpike road, which ran parallel to the tramroad, ceased to exist after conversion to a railway and Hollybush, like Argoed, had no main road up the valley at this time. Workmen living in the Tredegar and Argoed area's took a chance and still walked the lineside to Hollybush Colliery, many coming from Argoed before Abernant Colliery was sunk in 1888-89. Edmund Williams of Argoed started work at Hollybush Colliery when he was 13 years of age and walked both ways, doing 10 hour shifts. Later, he fired the boilers there, and was paid 22/- per week. Hollybush Colliery was bought by E. D. Williams of Maesruddud, near Argoed at a sale at the Westgate Hotel, Newport on the 9th October, 1868. The sale included machinery, Rolling stock, Tools and Stores. The total area of the mineral property was 80 acres, containing a seam called the

Pontygwaith & Marshall's vein and also fifty-five large coking ovens, a 10 h.p. steam engine with winding gear, and cast and wrought iron tramways. The Colliery was unique in some respects, as the coal came from the level mouth across on the east side of the river before coming up a shaft of one hundred and five feet. This was necessary to bring the coal up to a suitable height for tipping into the railway wagons. The only other example of this method was at Budd's Rock Colliery, Blackwood, where the men went in through the level mouth, but the coal came up a shaft of one hundred and seven feet near St. Margaret's Church. The pit ponies at Hollybush were well looked after and came out every weekend for grazing. After Mr. William's death in 1895, the Colliery continued under a trusteeship and executors, before its closure in about 1920.

There were shops down near the railway in the old part of Hollybush, and a Post Office where William Hicks was Subpostmaster, followed later by George Lewis in the 1930s. Other shops were situated in Springfield and Railway Terrace and some of them will be remembered—H. J. Fielding, Dorothy Griffiths, John Morgan, John Norwood, Charles Oliver and David Phillips; Ernest Brice, the Ironmonger, who had his shop on the New Road, will be remembered by many. Margaret Davies kept the Hollybush Inn and Joseph and Margaret Rogers occupied the Ancient Druid Beer House. The old school was under the control of Miss Lucy Ellis, but later, in 1914, a new school was built on the New Road at a cost of £4,200; the Master then was John Roxborough.

Mrs. Prior of Railway Terrace had a narrow escape in the later part of 1918 when a section of a large flywheel disintegrated at the Colliery and crashed through the roof of her house. Fortunately, no one was upstairs at the time and there were no injuries. A part of the flywheel, weighing several hundredweights, was lying around for many years after the incident.

Sport and Leisure

Rugby and Cricket was very popular. There was plenty of entertainments and concerts run chiefly by the Church and Chapels, particularly the Baptists who were very strong (the Chapel at Pontygwaith was erected in 1825). The old schoolroom became a Mission Hall under Bedwellty Church and in the old days Rector Roberts would go along the rows of houses, tapping the doors as he went along in an effort to get his flock to service! He was very well liked by all. The village also had its own library at this time.

The Ancient Druid is no longer a public house, but will be remembered for its association with Evan James and his family, and the Welsh National Anthem. The family moved several times, apparently coming here from Argoed; moving later to Aberbargoed, Nelson, and finally to Ynysddu before going to the Woollen Factory and house in Mill Street, Pontypridd.

Blackwood

The area which became known as the village of Blackwood was built on a natural shelf on the western side of the Valley. It had distinct advantages over Argoed, which was contained in a shallow basin. Many of the buildings were constructed alongside the Sirhowy Tramroad, as at Argoed. Principal landowners in the district were Sir Charles Morgan, J. H. Moggridge and E. D. Williams who leased the ground with mineral rights, to various prospectors; this led to many headings or levels being driven into the hillside and consequent need for men to work them. This, in turn, brought a large number of potential colliers into the district, all wanting somewhere to live. To meet this demand, houses began to appear very early in the 19th century. These levels were situated on each side of the river, extending from the Gelli to Libanus on the west side of the valley, and from Manmoel and Tŷr Philkins on the other.

In 1814 Edmund Williams of Maesruddud (E. D. Williams' father) agreed to let the marketable coals in the veins under his land to the Argoed & Newport Coal Company for a certain period at 1/- per ton royalty. This was the level in the wood above the quarry at Cwm Gelli, and David Lewis of Bedwellty agreed to let all marketable coals situated under lands belonging to Edward Lewis under a farm known as Gelli Dywyll, and called the Gelli Dywyll Coal Company. Cottages were built for the colliers, and the district became known as the Gelli.

In 1825, J. H. Moggridge of Woodfield, Blackwood, with Thomas Prothero and Thomas Powell, of St. Woolos, Newport agreed to lease for fifty-two years the coal in, upon and under a farm called Plas Bedwellty, together with the woodland commonly known as Blackwood, and also a farm called Cwm in Mynddislwyn for a rent of £356.5.0d a year, and also to work seams of coal now worked by the Rock and Penmaen Collieries. This important lease meant the opening of several collieries, one at Libanus, one between High Street and Lilian Road, known as Lower Plas Colliery, and another across the river at Cwm Filkins. These early collieries, and the relevant increase in housing for the workmen, formed the mainstay for the early development of Blackwood.

The report of a fatal occurrence at the Lower Plas Pit appeared in the 'Star of Gwent & South Wales Times' for Saturday, 27th January, 1872. It is typical of the graphic detail common in newspaper reports of the period:

'A most deplorable accident occurred on Thursday morning at 2 am at the Lower Plas Pit, Blackwood, which is being sunk by Messrs. Prothero. It appears that a number of men were employed at their night turns at sinking in the shored up sides of the Pit, and everything as usual appeared safe around them, when a shot was fired in the usual way, which must have shaken the timber uprights and supports for shortly after the explosion the whole gave way, and four men were, without warning, instantly buried and undoubtedly crushed to death. A few of those at work escaped, but one poor fellow named Tovey, who was standing on one of the beams when they all gave way, was unfortunately caught by the legs, and there held against the sides of the Pit. His cries were heartrendering as he called upon his comrades, and the crowd that flocked, even at that early hour to the pit's mouth to render him assistance. The pumping apparatus, having been destroyed, the water gradually increased and the poor fellow, whose legs were frightfully crushed, saw death not only staring him in the face, but surely advancing upon him. He besought the crowd to lower the chain and fasten it round his body and drag that up, even if his legs were left behind; but no assistance could be rendered. Gradually, the rubbish and debris that had fallen were covered by the water, and the poor fellow could see his span of life rapidly contracting as the water rose to the level at which he was lying. The scene was horrifying in the extreme. The pitiless element submerged the lower portions of his body, then his chest, and finally his head, hushing in death his unveiling cries for aid.

The names of the sufferers are as follows:—

William Treasure, 44, leaves a wife and seven children.
William Johnson, 34, leaves a wife and two children.
William Tovey, leaves a wife and two children.
Morgan Richards, 28, single.
William Poole, 27, single.

Dr. James and other medical men were quickly on the spot, but their services were not put into requisition. It is impossible at present to recover any bodies'.

According to a map of 1829, there were twenty-three houses on the western side of the tramroad and the river, and twenty on the Penmaen side. This amounted to a population of about 500 or more, making Blackwood the biggest town between Tredegar and Newport. Many of these early houses were built by David Evans. One of the early Inns—the 'Royal Oak' was leased to George Oliver, brewer of Newport as early as 1830. A market house, with public room was built and in use by October 1822.

In the days of the tramroad, (up to 1860), trucks would stop in front of the shops; one man, Morgan Morgans, regularly carried goods straight from the trucks to his shop! Morgans was a popular man and later became a carting agent for the Railway Company. In 1866 Mr. Chappell came to Blackwood to take over a grocery business; but by then the conversion from tramway through the main street, to railway at the back of the shops had taken place, so he did not enjoy the convenience available to Morgan Morgans! Business fell into decline in 1868 because of a coal strike which lasted sixteen weeks.

While on the subject of tramroads, an account of a boiler explosion at Blackwood is extracted from the 'Monmouthshire Merlin' for 23rd March, 1843:—

'On Saturday evening last at 5.30 pm as the Vulcan steam engine and trams (the property of the Tredegar Iron Company) was returning from Newport, when nearly opposite the George Inn, Blackwood, the boiler bursting and occasioned the lives of Mr. W. Davies, farmer, formerly of Buttery Hatch, and Mr. Phillip Jones, of Blackwood who was standing near the corner where the engine stood. Mr. Davies was upwards of 80 years old. All the glass was smashed in the George Inn. A man named James Hale who was standing on the footplate escaped injury as part of the boiler went over his head!

Samuel Homfray Esq., of Tredegar said all expenses would be met. Value of the Engine £500. Inquest held at Royal Oak, Blackwood, by W. Brewer Esq'.

The 'Vulcan' was not listed as a Tredegar built engine, but Sirhowy Railway engines, built later, came from the Vulcan Works at Warrington, which may have some relevant connection. The name 'Vulcan' also indicates a Smith or Ironworker.

The man who undoubtedly created a lasting impression on the early population of Blackwood was John Hodder Moggridge, born 1771 at Bradford on Avon, Wiltshire, where his mother's family were clothiers. The family moved afterwards to Dymock in Gloucestershire, and he became High Sheriff of that County in 1809, but later sold his property at Dymock and bought the Plas Bedwellty Estate (previously named Rhosnewydd) in the parishes of Bedwellty and Mynyddislwyn. He took a very active part in the social and political life of the district and introduced what he called his Village System. In return for a small ground rent, which was less than the customary cottage rent, Moggridge would lease ground to provide the capital to erect a substantial cottage from local stone with sufficient ground for a garden. The scheme was very successful and each year Moggridge met demands for more plots, and so it went on, until we come to the Blackwood depicted in some of the early Post Cards. Mr. Moggridge died at Swansea in 1834.

The Truck System

In reports to the Commissioners on the employment of children by R. H. Franks in 1842, a Blackwood Blacksmith, Joseph Thomas, stated that the truck system was so common in the local collieries that the markets were forced to close. In Blackwood, the whole supply was monopolised by the Company Shop.

Henry George, Innkeeper of Blackwood, had this to say: 'The effect of the truck system is remarkably developed in this Village. We have no Market, and in instances where the money is advanced at one end of the shop, it is laid out in goods at the other'. Bacon was 11d per lb; butter 1/1d per lb; candles 7d and cheese 7½d per lb.

The following description from a local woman called Sarah Tobay gives a warning as to the consequences of such a system:—

'I have eight children; four at work; my husband's wages, taking all things together, have not been 10/- a week all the year; though my husband gets his pay in cash, as he is favoured, but where one receives cash, thirty are compelled to deal at the shop—we have frequently been obliged to do so, and I am sure I can save 3/- in the pound by buying my own goods where I like, but those who are discontented are marked'.

Finally, we have another shopkeeper of Blackwood, Daniel Lewis who stated:—

'My shop is totally unconnected with any work or mine. The truck system has so injurious an effect on trade that our property and markets are destroyed, and the rent of the houses in Blackwood are not half of them paid. The system makes the poor class unhappy, by inducing which in itself is a dead drag on the wages of labour. You may depend on it, it will create a disturbance'.

The evils of child labour added to the misery of working class families. Seven year old William Richards detailed his work as an underground air-door boy:—

'I have been down about three years; I don't know my own age, when I first went down I couldn't keep my eyes open. I don't fall asleep now, I smoke my pipe, earns 8d a day. Never been to school, can't say what tobacco is made of, knows it comes from the shop, smokes half a quartern a week. Thinks mother pays 8d for half a quartern'.

(This little fellow was intelligent and good-humoured, his cap was furnished with the usual collier-candlestick, and his pipe was stuck familiarly in his button-hole).

Conversion from Tramroad to Railway

In 1860-61, during the conversion from tramroad to railway, with vignoles rails laid on chairs, a long embankment was made at the back of the shops on the eastern side from Libanus right up to the station, and bridges were made at Bridge Street, Hall Street (Hall Street was originally Sadler's Lane), and near Rock House for the Colliery Tramroad.

There were traces of early tramplates and stone blocks on the eastern side of the main street, which originally had no lighting—shops used candles, and the larger shops were lit by paraffin or gas. In the Libanus district was a cottage where Mr. W. James, the Hairdresser, carried on business; the garden in the front contained a Cherry Tree from which the cottage took its name. Mr. James was a noted musician and conductor for many years of the Blackwood Brass Band. Poplar trees covered the ground near to where the Blackwood Welfare Institute stands and there were oak, beech, ash and fir trees between Blackwood and Plas Farm; the area later consisted of houses in Gordon Road, Coronation Street, Albany Road and Woodbine Villas.

Blackwood Races

Local celebrities took part in most functions, including Blackwood Races. On the 11th June, 1870 upwards of 7,000 people attended the races. The prizes were distributed by Miss Williams, Maesruddud, (E. D. Williams' sister) and Lieutenant Stroud, a very popular Colliery Manager. According to the 'Monmouthshire Merlin', the Sirhowy Railway had their work cut out, as the entire resources of the carriage department were brought into requisition. In one or two instances a 'truck' was noticeable on the return journey and passengers were standing.

Explosion at Pochin Colliery

Mr. Harry Flower of Blackwood, who worked at Pochin Colliery cele-brated his nineteenth birthday by not going to work on that day. Fourteen men were killed in an explosion at the colliery. Philip Pugh, thought to be under the influence of drink, tried to help but fell down the shaft and was also killed. This disaster occurred in mid-November 1884. Mr. Flower recalled his lucky escape:—

> 'I had worked thirteen weeks without a day off, so decided not to go in'.

Mr. Flower's grandfather, who had died in the 1840s at 91 years of age, was a shoe-maker employed by Edmund Edmunds, Ironmonger, Saddle and Harness Maker, and also Postmaster at Blackwood, a business estab-lished as far back as 1828. Another Directory lists William Jones as Post-master and Sadler, Blackwood, in 1858. Mr. Flower remembers many fights taking place in a field near Morris Lane. There were only two policemen in Blackwood then and neither attempted to stop the fight— 'They wouldn't have dared', said Mr. Flower. Mr. Flower's father spoke of standpipes in use at various points in Blackwood in his day; when these dried up, water was taken from a spring near the Rock & Fountain Public House.

Schools

The Jerusalem British School at Woodfield opened in 1847. The Drill Hall at Blackwood was used as a temporary school, and its first Mistress, at a salary of £60 per year was Mrs. Jane Annie James, the wife of the local Police Sergeant, who was appointed on 8th September, 1873.

Her first class consisted of sixty-five pupils. She dismissed them for a week and opened again on the 15th September helped by Sarah Jenkins who had been a pupil teacher at the Jerusalem British School. The number in the class was then 73. A postscript added for 10th December, 1873 mentions that Elizabeth Garnett (aged 13 years) was expelled for beating the monitor.

It appears that the first purpose-built school in Blackwood was on Cefn Road, which opened on 28th May, 1877; the Headmaster then was Mr. Owen Edwards, a native of Snowdonia. The assistant teacher, Miss Evans was helped by two monitors, Cecilia Holder and Annie Rees. The school was named as Bedwellty Blackwood Council School No. 27 in 1909.

Examinations were held in June. No one in the second standard could spell 'trouble', 'shelter', or 'minute'; and standards 3 and 4 were very backward with writing, and arithmatic was disappointing. There was, however, a steady improvement as time went on, and as in most schools in the area at the time, half-day holidays were allocated for many local functions.

The building on Pentwyn Road was built about 1909 and opened by Dr. Howell Evans of the Laurels, Blackwood on Monday, 10th January 1910.

The contractors, however, refused entry to the building until County Hall was contacted and permission granted. The pupils were officially admitted on Wednesday, 12th January, 1910.

It seems the building on Cefn Road was refurbished and reopened on Monday, 21st November, 1910 as an infants' school, and remained so until closure in 1980, when the new infants' school in Apollo Way was opened.

Around this time (June 1910) it was recorded that there was serious over-crowding at the school, and so a temporary building was erected by 1912. It is still there to this day, serving as a canteen and three classrooms. By 1915 other schools in the area were completed, including those at Libanus and Cefn Fforest, and these new buildings were soon equipped and fully opera-tional. On 3rd January, 1916, Mr. Edwards, the Headmaster died; he passed away in hospital at Newport. He had been Headmaster for thirty-eight years.

Mr. Gomer Evans became the new Head and by 1923 the temporary building was used for technical classes. During the Second World War, fruit was tinned there.

Mr. R. E. Hough became Headmaster of the Elementary School; he had been at Argoed as Head for many years (followed Frank Parsons at Argoed) but went to Libanus as Headmaster in 1934 and retired on 31st January, 1940.

About 1946, the whole site became Blackwood Secondary Modern School (Headmaster, Mr. Griffiths) which also had a small annexe in Cefn Road used for domestic science classes. From this date there appears to have been no Junior School in Blackwood because pupils attended either

Libanus or Cefn Fforest School. About 1957, the new Secondary Modern School was built near the Show Field.

Libanus School

This school was opened on 1st July, 1915 and given the name of Libanus Council School, Blackwood. The first pupils were admitted on 5th July, 1915. The Headmaster was Frank Parsons. The school log book was recently made available by Mrs. Janet Morris, the present Head, and it reveals in detail all aspects of the school's running over the years. In December 1929 a sum of £5 was left to the school by Mr. Thomas Sambrook Jones for the purpose of buying gramophone records. They were purchased from F. Templeman, a Blackwood business man for many years.

During the 1921 Coal Strike, arrangements were made for feeding necessitous children. This started on 22nd April of that year and finished on 22nd July, by which time 6,508 dinners had been served! School meals were continued again from 24th January, 1919 to 8th May, 1931, when a total of 14,000 meals were served.

A 'good attendance' half-day holiday is recorded on 10th July, 1931; but 1935 was indeed, a sad year for the school when two children were drowned in fifteen feet of water at a disused quarry at the back of the school. Mr. R. E. Hough took Mr. Parson's place as Head in 1934.

The school closed for a few weeks in 1939 for A.R.P. Training, and the first Air Raid Practice took place in September. The school day was shortened to 10.00-12.15, and 1.30-3.30 in 1940. Three stirrup pumps and six fire buckets for fire-watching were delivered, and the first air raid alert took place in March of that year.

During the blizzard of 1947, the school was closed from approximately 30th January to 4th March, and again from 5th to 11th March, no doubt with delight by all the children! Mr. J. E. Jarman became Headmaster in 1940.

At one time a private fee-paying school existed in Blackwood. The school was run by Miss Hyatt at Oakland Place, Cefn Road, later moving to Linwood. It was taken over by an excellent teacher called Mrs. Jenkins. The school moved again to The Lindens in South View, where Mrs. Jenkins taught music and trained pupils for public speaking. The school was still operating in 1932, and catered for Young Ladies and Gentlemen, but sometimes retarded children were also taught there.

The Baptists at Blackwood
MOUNT PLEASANT CHURCH

The first building was the Welsh Baptists Church at Libanus, which is shown on the 1860 map; but an effort was made as early as 1861 to establish an English Baptist cause at Blackwood. They met first in the old Wesleyan Chapel, and by November 1861, nine members were formed into a church, and a fairly numerous Sunday School was organised. Because of the dilapidated state of the old Chapel, a move was made to the schoolroom attached to Jerusalem, the Welsh Congregational Chapel. However, a very serious strike occurred in the district, and members had to seek work in other localities, and many moved with their families, with the result that the promising church now practically became extinct. The strike over, many came back from the surrounding districts to Blackwood and services began again on Sunday, 14th May, 1876 in the house of Mr. Evan Bowen in Dandy Row when Mr. J. Whitton Davies, (later Professor J. Whitton Davies, B.A., Ph.D., M.R.A.D., University College, Bangor) preached, being a student at Pontypool College then.

The house soon became too small, and a Clubroom connected with the Parrot Hotel was rented. In June 1879, services were removed from the Clubroom to the Chapel of Ease at Cwmygelly, and later, in 1881 a Schoolroom was completed and opened for divine service at a total cost of £350.

During the pastorship of William Ingli James of Nantgwyn, Radnorshire, a Chapel was built capable of seating 600 at the north end of the Schoolroom; galleries were at each side and in front of the rostrum, and a beautiful pipe-organ was installed at a cost of £1,500.

On Sunday, 2nd October, 1910 at a meeting of members of the church, the Rev. John Bage of Chester was appointed pastor; the terms were 'That a salary be £120 per annum and that leave of absence shall be four Sundays per year, and should you be absent from the pulpit upon any other date, that you shall provide a substitute approved by the officers of the church'.

On 11th December, 1911, Mr. A. Richards gave a 'Notice of Motion' for the next church meeting in the following terms: 'That the Deacons, to be in keeping with the democratic spirit of the age, and to obliterate officialdom which is evidently a curse to Nonconformity, be requested to sit in the body of the church and should make themselves active by way of looking out for strangers and extend a welcome to them'. This sentiment seemed to have had very little support amongst the general body of church members, and the elderly deacons continued to occupy the 'big seat' for many years.

The Rev. John Bage resigned from the pastorate in March 1913. On 14th September, 1914, it was proposed by Mr. Chas Williams, and seconded by Mr. A. Richards 'that we secure a house at the Garden City (Cefn Fforest) which will be tenantable to hold a Prayer Meeting and services to form the nucleus of a mission to be started up there'. This suggestion resulted in the formation of Bethany Baptist Chapel at Cefn Fforest.

In October 1915, the Rev. W. O. William of Builth Wells accepted the Pastorship at Blackwood—a ministry which he occupied for the next twenty-five years, although the Rev. Williams continued to serve the church regularly after his retirement in 1940. It was a momentous period in the history of Mount Pleasant, for the Minister arrived during the 1914-18 war and saw his congregation, many of whom were miners, battle through the 1921 and 1926 strikes, during which the schoolroom was used as a Soup Kitchen.

The church received more than 190 new members by Baptism, a Full Band of Hope session every autumn and winter for many years, and an exceedingly strong Young People's Society that had a marked influence on the lives of the large numbers who attended.

In the early part of the century, each denomination followed its Anniversary with its own Sunday School treat on Monday, but later, all denominations paraded together on Whitsun Monday and the Show field became the venue for the Sports and Games which followed the tea.

The Rev. T. H. Hill, B.A., B.D., of Cardiff followed the Rev. W. O. Williams and commenced his Ministry in September 1944. In February 1953, the Rev. Hill went to Siloh Church, Tredegar as Pastor there and his place was taken by the Rev. Vaughan Walters, B.A. Mr. Walters had spent the previous fifteen years in India and in July 1963, accepted an assignment with the British & Foreign Bible Society, leaving Mount Pleasant again without a Minister.

The Rev. Haydn James, B.A., B.D. of Aberystwyth took up the Ministry in February 1965, resigning in March 1972. The present Minister, the Rev. R. J. Young, B.A., has been with the Church since August 1973.

The Choirmaster in the early days was Mr. Edwin Jones, of Pengam, but in 1915 Mr. George James was appointed as Conductor, and became actively engaged with the music of the church as Conductor and Organist for many years. There were others engaged at various times as Conductors, Organists and Choirmasters, including Mr. Thomas Norman, Mr. V. Norman, Mr. Thomas Davies and Mr. Stanley Jones.

Methodism in Blackwood

The earliest Methodists in Blackwood met in a cottage, now demolished, near St. Margaret's Church. Later, another cottage was used (the old Crown Inn) which stood in Blackwood High Street on the site now occupied by Tesco's Supermarket. There was no chapel built until 1834, when the first of five chapels, to be built over the years, was erected on the site now occupied by St. Margaret's Church. This building accommodated 100 people, and the money was advanced by a Mr. Jones, of Rock House.

No sooner was the first chapel completed than it was realised more room was needed, and a new site near the centre was obtained, now occupied by the car park at the rear of the present Central Methodist Church.

The granting of this site was regarded as a triumph, since Lewis Lewis, the owner, one of the principal coal magnates of the time, was quite averse to letting his land for building purposes—'More things are wrought by prayer than this world dreams of', Abraham Coleman, one of the Methodist pioneers of his time, and one of the most remarkable characters Methodism has ever known, prayed on his knees in a nearby wood, whilst

John Waters, another pioneer, approached the landlord for the land purchase. Abraham Coleman—'God gave the Land'.

John Waters supervised the building and in 1861, the second Wesleyan Chapel was opened, seating 200, and aptly named Perseverance in recognition of the dedicated efforts of the members.

Incidentally, Abraham Coleman and John Waters preached regularly in the open air on the Square at Blackwood at this time. Other faithful workers were David Tucker, Samuel Coleman (Abraham's son), James Nethercott, William Tucker, J. F. Chappel, James Sumption and James Coleman—these will be recognised as Blackwood businessmen of the past.

The third Wesleyan Chapel was built in 1898 on the site of 'Perseverance' to accommodate a congregation of 630. The cost was £1,250 and members gave both labour and money towards the building. Many men, after their day's work in the Pit, would spend every available hour helping to excavate and prepare the site.

In the early 1900s Blackwood had 150 members, and the Chapel had a large Sunday School, a Band of Hope, and a Wesley Guild. Two other men connected with the Chapel at this time were the Rev. J. H. Morgan, who later held the office of President of the Manitoba Methodist Conference, and the Rev. William Coleman (son of Samuel Coleman and grandson of Abraham Coleman) who was accepted into the ministry of the Methodist Episcopal Church of America.

In 1904 an Evangelistic Mission was held in Blackwood under the leadership of the Rev. A. D. Baskerville, the Blackwood Minister from 1903 to 1905. The Quarterly Love Feasts were also occasions of great spiritual uplift—the hearty miners delighting in singing the old Gospel Songs, giving spontaneous testimony and uttering joyous shouts of praise—the spiritual leaders again were David Tucker, James Coleman, James Nethercott, Solomon Davies, George Head and Harry Tucker.

During the First World War, in 1915, the third Wesleyan Chapel in Blackwood was destroyed by fire, the cause of which has never been established. Rebuilding took place immediately, the fourth Wesleyan Chapel being erected on the same site. The fifth Wesleyan Chapel was erected in front of the fourth chapel and officially opened on the 1st March, 1928. The cost of the building was £12,000. There was a transfer of members of the Primitive Methodist cause at the Rehoboth Chapel in Woodbine Road— this chapel is now the Little Theatre.

The preacher at the opening service of the new chapel was the Rev. Dr. Luke Wiseman, and the first christening was that of Mary Groves, daughter of Mr. Gordon Groves.

A generous donation by Mr. David Tucker in 1944 resulted in the fine Pipe Organ installed in the church—older members will recall Mr. George Coleman, organist and choirmaster, with his white beard and tuning fork. He was succeeded by Mr. D. M. Williams.

George Head was a Methodist—a familiar figure in the Blackwood district and also the local Argus Reporter. He was one of the first to establish a Reading Room at Blackwood.

There are interesting stories about Abraham Coleman, who died 11th May, 1878. The following are extracted from a booklet entitled:—

METHODISM IN BLACKWOOD—
150 Years Anniversary—1834-1984.

'He was a mighty man in prayer, in wayside hedges, in woods and fields, while the dew lay sparkling on the grass, in snow and rain, and when the deepening shadows were falling over the valley, at all times and seasons he was wont to kneel in prayer whenever led thereto by the spirit. He was revered by all. On one occasion, a professed infidel lay dying, and the medical attendant asked if he should send for the Vicar of the Parish, "No, I am as good as he", "Shall I send for Abraham Coleman?" "Yes", said the infidel, "he is a good man".'

The second extract is shown below:—

'At another time, through bad trade and hard times, things were going behind, and on the Saturday night, Abraham said to his wife, "Sarah, thou know'st my toes are out through my boots, and the weather be bad and I have to preach tomorrow, go to the shop for a pair of boots". Sarah went and stated her case. The Shopkeeper refused to send the boots. Being determined to fulfil his appointment on the morrow, Abraham told all to God. Rising early in the morning, he found the boots hanging on the latch of the door. The Shopkeeper had had no rest till the required boots were taken, but as it was late at night, he had left them hung on the latch".

The Ministers and dates are as follows:—

Rev. W. James	— 1891-1892
Rev. J. Wells	— 1895-1898
Rev. George Hooper	— 1898-1900
Rev. Benjamin Nume	— 1900-1901
Rev. Edward Harris	— 1901-1903
Rev. A. D. Baskerville	— 1903-1905
Rev. H. Baird Turner	— 1905-1908
Rev. Ernest Boulton	— 1908-1912
Rev. George Glandfield	— 1912-1914
Rev. Robert Ellison	— 1914-1918
Rev. H. J. Dixon	— 1918-1921
Rev. C. W. Martin	— 1921-1925
Rev. George Burden	— 1925-1928
Rev. George Grieve	— 1928-1931
Rev. E. Tegryd Davies	— 1931-1942
Rev. Thomas Bate	— 1942-1946
Rev. G. S. B. Knapp	— 1946-1951
Rev. Ernest R. Pickard	— 1951-1954
Rev. Stephen Gibson	— 1954-1956
Rev. T. Laverick Wilson	— 1956-1960

Rev. Harold Sharratt — 1960-1965
Rev. F. S. Pritchard — 1965-1970
Rev. George Daniels — 1970-1973
Rev. Brinley Griffiths — 1973-1976
Rev. Leslie Stephenson — 1976-1978
Rev. Margaret Stanworth — 1978-1983
Rev. A. H. Gledhill — 1983-1987
Rev. D. H. Howarth — 1987-

Shops and Businesses

The older inhabitants would remember many business people of the town—the Colemans—Odabiah, the newsagent; Abraham, the grocer; and George Coleman, a noted music teacher. Sydney Godwin, outfitter; J. V. Lewis (John Vinson), grocer and two very well-known Blackwood men—Cromwell Jones and George Nethercott. There were also the familiar business names of the valley towns: Home and Colonial; India and China Tea Co., Peglers Stores and Scudamore & Co.; also Sumption Bros., the very obliging chemists in Blackwood, and Mr. Chappell, the grocer. In 'Kelly's 1914 Directory', Alfred Chaston is listed as a Plumber, High Street, Blackwood, but later established a very successful business. Longstaffs had a Penny Bazaar in the High Street. Post cards of local views were very popular with the public in the period 1890-1920 and thousands were sold; some newsagents had them printed for them—Odabiah Coleman and J. H. Murrin in Blackwood and J. Phillips in Argoed.

Weather

Blizzards of the past are recorded here—in 1921 there was a complete stoppage on road and rail in April. Eleven passengers were rescued from a train between Argoed and Hollybush and the braziers used for preventing the water from freezing at the stations were not effective, thus curtailing the use of locomotives.

Dr. Howell Evans, of the Laurels, at the Gelli, going to Bedwellty on his rounds in December 1925, found the snow over nine feet deep in places, and over the hedges—two horses failed to remove his car and it had to be left. The following day they found footprints where people had walked over it without knowing. Remember 'Joe, the Doctor?' Well, he was the Doctor's chauffeur and handyman.

Weatherwise, many will recall the icy winter of 1940, with trains trapped for up to thirty hours on the Sirhowy Line and buses stranded at peculiar angles across the main road in many places. The telephone wires were covered in a thick layer of ice; the weight eventually bringing them down, breaking four of the poles off at about six feet from ground level in the vicinity of Sunny View, Argoed; the area extending from the Primitive Methodists' Chapel to Fairoak. Many other poles were down at various places in the Valley. This occurred on Sunday and Monday, the 28th and 29th January, 1940. Electricity was off for twenty hours and there were no papers until 4.00 p.m. on the Monday. Following this, the Chester Division of the Post Office Engineering Department were assisting in repairs for some time.

The winters of 1947 and 1962-63 were severe; snow started to fall on the last day of December 1962 and continued for several weeks. It was, indeed, unparalleled for sheer quantity of snow and disruption to traffic.

Businesses and well-known Personalities at Blackwood

James Edgar Roberts (Roberts, the Printer) started in Blackwood in 1908 at 93 High Street. In 1914 he moved to 91 High Street, and was known later as 'The Sirhowy Valley Printing Works'.

The original Gas Works, owned by Mr. Morris, was situated behind the present Woolworth's building, and Woolworth's was built on the site of the house occupied by Mr. Edmund Edmunds, mentioned earlier. The new Gas Works, near the Rock & Fountain Public House, was opened on 9th July, 1891, and was again under the management of this gentleman. He came to Blackwood from Llanelly at the age of 15 and was apprenticed to his Uncle, Roger Davies, in the grocery trade. Morris Lane is named after him, and he was responsible for Blackwood's first street lighting.

There was a lodging house in Blackwood run by Mr. William Ebley, and to get to it you went down Hall Street, and after passing under the railway, you turned left.

Councillors for Blackwood in 1910 were Peter Coleman, Sydney Godwin and Henry Pope. The Curate at St. Margaret's Church (Chapel of Ease to Bedwellty) was the Rev. Ernest Tyfaelog Theophilus, B.A., and the Post-mistress at this time was Miss Lucy Watkins.

Entertainment—Theatres and Cinemas

The Rink in Blackwood was a large corrugated iron building standing near the Bon Marche. It was also called the Pavilion Theatre and used for weekend Youth Drama Festivals. The exit opened onto Cefn Road, whilst the entrance was reached by a long flight of wooden steps from the main road, on the pavement of which the Manager, Edgar Hopkins, who would walk up and down, inviting passers-by to 'Walk-up, Walk-up, seats guaranteed in all parts, 3d, 6d, 9d and one shilling!'.

It was used as a cinema in the 1920s, where I saw many of the silent films. Just above, on the other side of the road was the Palace Cinema, standing somehwere near Babers present shop. Alfred Thompson was the Manager. While on the subject of theatres, we must not forget the Blackwood Amateur Dramatic Society, founded in 1921 by Mrs. Charlotte Powell, and incidentally, Blackwood has links with the Fabian Society; among its many distinguished members were Beatrice and Sidney Webb, who were pioneers in exposing the Poor Law system at the time. The Senior Citizen's Home at Blackwood takes its name after her.

All the railway crossings over the main road have gone—the one at the Rock (Primrose Colliery) also Upper Cwm Gelli, near the farm, and Lower Cwm Gelli siding, which turned up near Dr. Evans residence. The crossing at Libanus has also long disappeared. J. E. Trehearne's Rock Foundry, near the bottom of the Foundry Hill, established in 1823 is no longer there, and there is no trace now of the Budd's Rock Colliery and siding near St. Margaret's Church, where I saw the railway engine picking up loaded coal wagons on many occasions, with a Flagman to control the road traffic!

The Bedwellty Show Day—on the first Monday in September (Mabon's Day) was, and still is, a very busy day for Blackwood, and up to about 1935 most of the long-distance traffic came by rail to Blackwood Yard and you would see the endless trail of horses going up Foundry Hill to the Show Ground. Special trains were run and a portable Booking Office was fixed at the top end of the up platform for booking Newport passengers.

The first Bedwellty Show was held at the Penllwyn in 1873 when Mrs. Bevan, of Argoed Fawr Farm gained a first prize for the best bull entered. Another winner at the Show was E. L. Jenkins, Argoed Farm (Argoed Uchaf). He won on several occasions in husbandry and also won the Shire Horse Society 'Silver Medal'.

The Show Day has now been changed to a Saturday in mid-August.

There were, of course, those sounds unforgettable (with apologies to Wynne Calvin, BBC Radio Wales), the little coal tank engine shunting in Blackwood Yard, and the goods van detached from the rear of the 11.50 a.m. Newport passenger at Gelli Signal Box and propelled into the yard, again by the same shunting engine. Who could forget that shrill, high-pitched 'North Western' whistle of the 'Coal' Tank Engines. The vans often contained Crawford's biscuits, Farm produce and fresh fruit or the odd van of salt for Mr. Hughes—known by everyone as Sammy Salt! Crawford's rented a part of the railway goods shed at Blackwood. The pace was casual and leisurely, and very peaceful then.

Appendix

INTERESTING DIRECTORY ENTRIES FOR THE AREA

I

Slater's Directory of Berkshire, Monmouthshire, and North and South Wales—June 1844.

Tredegar—Nail Makers (4) One—Elizabeth Griffiths.

Taverns and Public Houses.

    Mary Saunders, Church House, Bedwellty

    Joseph Holmes, New Inn, Bedwellty

    Richard Evans, Argoed Arms Public House

    William Price, Castle Public House and Miller (Water).

Lascelles & Co's Directory & Gazetteer, County of Monmouth, 1852.

Bedwellty Special & Petty Sessions. Wednesday; once a month at Rock Inn, Bedwellty.

Rev. Edmund Leigh, Clergyman of Bedwellty, Myrtle Grove, Blackwood.

Captain Henry Godfrey Marsh, Rock, Blackwood.

E. D. Williams, Maesruddud.

William Williams, Maesruddud.

Mr. William Ion, Bedwellty.

Ann Edmunds, Blacksmith, Argoed.

Thomas Ellis, Sen., Civil Engineer, Charles Street, Tredegar.

John Evans, Beer Retailer, Argoed.

David Hopkins, Tea Dealer, Argoed.

David Hopkins, Miller, Argoed.

Matthew Ion, Farmer, Rhoswen.

Eliza James, Beer Retailer and Woollen Manufacturer, Cymreigyddion House, Argoed, Bedwellty.

S. G. James, Farmer, Tynewydd, Bedwellty.

Isaac Jenkins, Blacksmith, The Rock, Blackwood.

Mary Lloyd, Argoed Arms, Argoed.

David Thomas, Blacksmith, Bedwellty.

II

Henry Thomas, Tailor, Bedwellty.
Mrs. Elenor Treherne, Ironfounder, Blackwood.
Evan Treherne & Co., Ironfounders, Blackwood.
John M. Waters, Bridge Inn, Argoed.
Watkin Watkins, Carpenter, Rock, Blackwood.
J.P.s—Henry Marsh
        T. Llewellyn Brewer.
Church of England Service is performed at the School, Court-y-bella (*sic*),
    Rev. Rees Jones, Minister—Service 11 a.m. & 6 p.m.
William Joseph Davies, Surgeon, Pennar House.
Roger Lewis, Coal Agent, Gwrhay.

Monmouthshire Poll Book—1847.
Aberystruth.
Rock Inn, Bedwellty.
William Duggins, Argoed.
Isaac Edwards, Cwmcorrwg.
Thomas Evans, Argoed.
John Fothergill, Cefnrychdir.
Charles George, Argoed Genol.
John Hopkins, Argoed Genol.
Matthew Ion, Rhoswen.
David James, Cwmcorrwg.
Isaac Jenkins, Argoed.
John Jones, Rock Shop
Henry Marsh, Grosvenor Place, Bath.
Henry Godfrey Marsh, Rock Cottage.

III

Matthew Moggridge, Woodfield
Gregory Perrot, Pencoed.
William Perrott, Hengoed.
Morgan Rees, Bedwellty.
Thomas Thomas, Sen., Argoed.
Thomas Thomas, Jun., Argoed.
David Treherne, Rock Foundry.
John Walters, Argoed.
Watkin Watkins, Argoed.
Edmund Williams, Maesruddud.
James Yorath, Newport.

Slater's 1850 Directory
Clawrplwyf—Hamlet.
Joseph Beaumont, Tump House.
Christmas Evans, Gelligroes.
John Leyshon, Rhiw Syr Dafydd.
William Lewis, Waterloo.
Roger Lewis, Gwrhaivawr.
Lewis Rochard, Nr. Court-y-bellow (sic).
Watkin Watkins, Gwrhai Vach.
James Walters, Cwm Corrwg.
Slater's 1880 Directory.
Postmaster, Blackwood, Edmund Edmunds.
G. J. James, J.P., Tynewydd.
Rev. Rees Jones, Myrtle Grove.

IV

William Llewellin, J.P., Woodfield House.
Edmund Williams, J.P., Maesruddud.
Court-y-bela, (Sir Thomas Phillips).
Henry Loftus Munroe, Master.
Eliza Munroe, Mistress.
John Dalby, The Rock, Blacksmith.
Daniel Jones, Argoed.
Bevan & Price, Rhoswen Colliery.

Woollen Manufacturers

Catherine John—Cwm Corwy.
William Price—Cwm Corwy.
Thomas Tuck—Cwm Corwy.
Argoed Baptists—Rev. Evan George.

Millers

James Moore, Gelligroes.
William Price, Cwmcorwy.

Farmers

Mrs. Bevan, Argoed.
George Coggins, Blackwood.
Matthew Ion, Rhoswen.
John Morgan, Blackwood.
Richard Morris, Blackwood.

Price Bevan, Courtcoch.
Edmund Edmunds, Blackwood.
Mrs. Llewellyn, Hafodtrisclod.
William Morgan, Argoed.
William Price, Argoed.

Morris & Co's Commercial Directory of Hereford and Monmouthshire—1862.
Blackwood—Rev. Rees Jones, Myrtle Grove.
Captain Marsh, J.P.
Francis Moggridge—Agent.

V

Mr. Henry Loftus Monroe—Court-y-bella.
L. W. Williams, Esq., Maesyrhyddid (sic)
S. H. Yorkney, Civil Engineer, Woodfield.
James Askil, Farmer.
Mary Roberts, Flannel Dealer.
Rock Colliery Co.—Mr. John Jones, Manager.

Kelly's 1910 Directory

Urban District Council. Argoed Ward.
William Bufton. Phillip L. Lloyd.
Medical Officer of Health—Howel Thomas Evans.
Schools: Manmoel (mixed) built 1880. Miss G. M. Hussey, Mistress.
Argoed P.O. Elizabeth Margaret Evans, Sub-Postmistress.
Public Elementary School, Mixed and Infants, built 1889, enlarged 1906.
Frank Parsons, Master. Miss E. A. Price, Mistress.
Station Master, Frank Reynolds.
Police—Henry Fearis.

Places of Worship

Bedwellty (St. Sannan)—Rev. William Roberts, Rector.
Argoed Baptists (Welsh and English)—Rev. David Morgan.
Calvinistic Methodists (Rock) (Welsh and English)—Rev. Roderick
    Morgan.
Primitive Methodists (Argoed) Rhymney Valley Circuit—Rev. William
    Tootel.

Commercial

Arth Bunston. Boot Dealer, Leicester House.
George Doidge, Builder. Frederick Giles, 8 Sunny View, Shopkeeper.

VI

Arthur Samuel Haines, Grocer.
Mrs. William Harris, Argoed Farm.
Rosser Isaac Jenkins, Grocer. John Jones, Cabinet Maker.
Phillip Lloyd, Argoed Arms P.H.
David Meredith, Shopkeeper. David Morgan, Ironmonger.
William Morgan, Butcher. William Morgan, Farmer.
William Morgan, Lodging House Keeper.
William O'Connor, Colliery Manager, Bargoed Coal Co., Abernant.
James Phillips, Hairdresser.
Walter Thomas Phillips, Solicitor.
Thomas Norman Price, Architect.
Richard Richards, Farmer, Argoed Ganol.
Edwin Robinson, Shopkeeper.
John Thomas, Boot and Shoe Maker.
Thomas Williams, Builder.

ROCK

Moses Heal, Grocer.
William Morgan, Blacksmith.
Mrs. E. Padfield, Midwife.

Penmain, including Court-y-bella

The Church of St. Philip & James, erected in 1855—a small edifice in the
Gothic style.
Rev. David Gower, Vicar. Curate, Rev. Lewis David Richards.
Welsh Congregational Chapel founded in 1639. Rev. Robert Evans.
Moses Walters, Preswylfa. Thomas Jones, Farmer, Penderry.
Mrs. Mary Evans, Woollen Manufacturer.

VII

Richard Evans, Coffee Tavern, Cross Penmain.
Mrs. Merium Lewis, Farmer and Colliery Owner, Gwrhay Fach.
Edwin Lloyd, Tyr Sais.

The
Photographs

1 Tyr-Philkins Colliery Site.

This single mineral line branches off the Western Valleys railway near Cross Keys and comes up through Penar Tunnel, terminating at Markham Colliery. Benjamin Hall was instrumental in the making of it as a tramway in 1805; known as Hall's

2   Early group at Woodfield Colliery

3   View of the Rock Inn, also Rock Calvinistic Methodist Chapel, built in 1824 (top right). Long wall in foreground was built by Tom Williams, Argoed in 1897. Garage was owned by Mr. Meredith, the carpenter, at one time. There was a Meeting House on the extreme left of the picture near the road before the Chapel was erected. The Rock Inn was an important place years ago for Council Meetings and Petty Sessions for the Bedwellty District

Photo by Cyril Jones, Argoed

5 Another view of Primrose Colliery at the Rock. Main road looking towards Argoed. Old road went sharp left behind wall. Track is seen from screens across road to siding on right, from where the loaded wagons were picked up by the railway engine

4 Primrose Colliery, Rock (not to be confused with New Rock Colliery (Budds) at Blackwood). There were three screens on the roadside near the Rock Inn. Owner was Christopher Pond, but Colliery worked by Love & Gittins before closure

6 Print showing second stack at Oakdale

7 Gwrhay and Cwrt-y-bela. Top right—Daren Felen Farm

8 Ty-Melin—Site of Oakdale Colliery. Also spelled Tymellyn

9 Sinking Operations at Oakdale Colliery. 1907-10. 726 yards

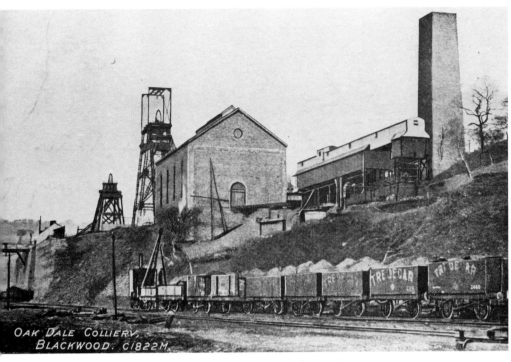

10 Oakdale Colliery soon after sinking

11 Oakdale Colliery soon after completion

12   Oakdale Colliery from the Parsons Bridge

13   Old River Bridge at Argoed over Sirhowy River

4 Old Cottage (now demolished) near Pont-yr-Dafydd at the Rock. Mentioned by Arch-eacon Coxe in his book entitled 'An Historical our in Monmouthshire'. Published in two volumes, 1801

5 Cwrt-y-bela and Barnes Siding

Cwtyrbella Church near Oakdale.

16   Cwm Corrwg, Argoed. One of the best prints showing the Castle Public House. Main Flannel Factory Building behind and, on extreme lower right, part of the old Corn Mill. In middle distance is Island Street, not long completed, and top left, Cwrt-y-bela School

17   Cwm Corrwg as it is today, showing in foreground all that remains of original buildings. The Cwm Bridge has evidently had a face-lift!   *Photo by Cyril Jones, Argoed*

18 Argoed High Street—1905-10. Post Office and J. Phillips (Jim, the Barber) shop on the right. Background right, Jediah Thomas's Butchers Shop. Left foreground, Reading Room and Library. This Post Card sold and specially printed for Jim Phillips, Stationer, Argoed

19 Another Post Card of Argoed Village

High Street.   Argoed.

20 Argoed Village in the 1920's showing shops and Argoed Arms Hotel (Phil Lloyd, Proprietor) on left. Part of Station House and Lodging House on near right

21 View near Fair Oak, with Fair Oak Farm extreme left (once a Beer House) and Round House (was, in fact, square) in foreground. The Cwm and Castle Hotel in middle distance

22 Argoed Station, built 1878—one of the best station buildings on the line, with a typical 'North Western' verandah

23 Cwm Road and James Street, Cwm

24 Gelynos Avenue, Argoed

25 Footpath from Storehouse to Fairoak under railway embankment. Fair Oak Farm House in distance

26 Snow Scene, above Argoed. April 1921

27 Photograph taken 24th August, 1937 of accident near Sunny View spout, Argoed. Sunny View Tip in background (Cwm Crach Colliery) levelled off in 1950 by Birmingham Contractors. People on right foreground are Mr. Jim Lloyd (near fence) and Mr. Buffery

28 Sunny View, Argoed. 1905-10 period. Fingerpost long disappeared shows Bedwellty, Argoed Village, Blackwood and Tredegar. On extreme right, at end of railings, was Sunny View spout, where queues formed for water, during a drought

29 One of Christopher Pond's early wagons—he lived in Blackwood. Note spelling of 'Manmole'. He owned levels at Gwaelodywain, Gelli, Penyfan, and Primrose at the Rock

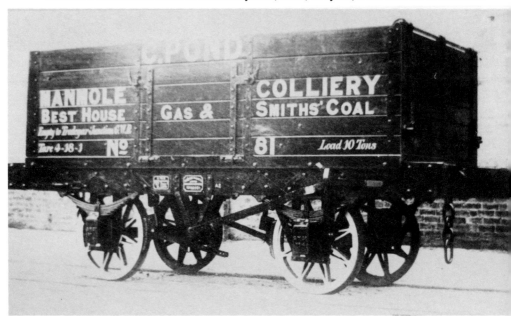

30 Argoed Signal Box. Signalmen here years ago included Harry Black and Tom Porter

31 Parson's Bridge, Argoed (now demolished), 1987

Courtesy of Cyril Jones, Argoed

32 Trip to Porthcawl from Argoed. Vehicle owned and driven by Gurnos Harris, second left

33 Early Argoed Outing—William Harris' charabanc

COURTYBELLA CHURCH   35452

34 Cwrt-y-bela Church. Dedicated to Saints Philip and James—the surname of Sir Thomas and his wife's maiden name. The first Minister, the Rev. Rees Jones, lived at Myrtle Grove, Blackwood. The Church was built in 1857. The last service was held in April 1969. The Church once had a choir of forty!

35 Rev'd John Jenkins,
Minister at Argoed Baptist Chapel

36 & 37 Argoed Cricket Team

38 Thomas Phillips (later Sir Thomas). Print taken after injury at Westgate Hotel, Newport in the 1839 Chartist Riots. He was Mayor of Newport in 1839

39 Barn at Argoed Fawr Farm, 1936

40 Rock Chapel

Photo by Cyril Jones, Argoed

41 Cwrt-y-bela School Class of Girls. Mr. & Mrs. Munroe believed to be on right, and the Rev'd Rees Jones, second left

42 School Class in the 1860's

43 Boys' class and Staff. Cwrt-y-bela school. 1870

44 Early car at Libanus, Blackwood (believed to be Rexette) owned by Mr. Edmund Williams, Argoed, sitting on back

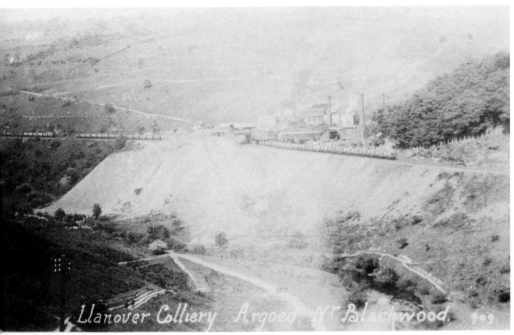

45 Llanover Colliery, Argoed. Manager in 1916—Edwin Rosser, Bargoed Coal Company

46 Abernant-y-felin, nr. Argoed, showing part of viaduct taking railway
to Markham Colliery

47 Markham Colliery nearing completion in 1912

48 Markham Colliery—drawn from Markh
Village Signal Box in June 1930   *W. W. Ta*

49 Markham Village Signal Box. Signalmen in the early days were James Bradford and John Thomas, followed later by Charlie Thomas and Sam Sandford   *Courtesy of Gerald Davies*

50   Hillside Avenue, Abernant Road, Markham Village

51 Welfare Hall, Markham Village

52 The station, Hollybush, about 1905   *Courtesy of C. J. R. Wilson*

53 Abernant Colliery, near Argoed

Courtesy of C. J. R. Wilson

54 The Colliery, Hollybush

Courtesy of C. J. R. Wilson

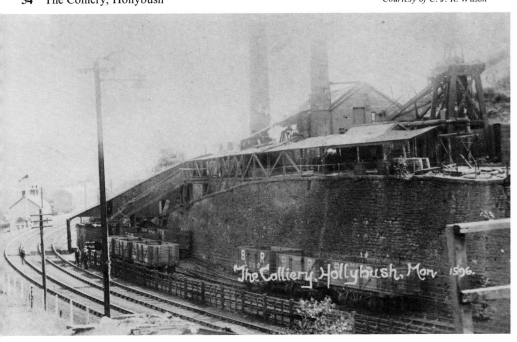

55 & 56 Colliers at Hollybush

57 Llwynbach Terrace, Hollybush

58 Hollybush Colliery. Bought by E. D. Williams at the Westgate Hotel, Newport in 1868

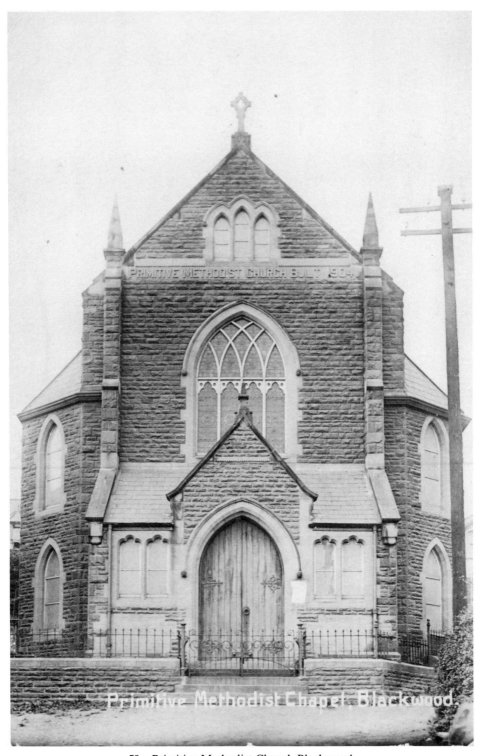

59 Primitive Methodist Chapel, Blackwood.
Now the 'Little Theatre'

60 & 61   High Street, Blackwood

62 & 63   High Street, Blackwood

64 High Street, Blackwood

65 High Street, Blackwood. Old underground toilet on right

66 Coach & Horses Public House, Blackwood. Headquarters for Chartists (Blackwood area). Demolished 1958

67 Interior Bedwellty Church

Restoration of
Bedwellty
Parish Church,
to
commemorate
the Coronation
of
King Edward VII
1902.

By . . .
JOHN BRIND.

AUTHOR OF

"Marmon Hall,"

"Short History of the
Church,"

Etc., Etc., Etc.

History

OF

Bedwellty
Church.

NEWPORT, MON.,
R. H. Johns, Printer, &c., Directory Office.
MDCCCCII.

68   Cover, History of Bedwellty Church, 1902

The Restoration of Bedwellty Parish Church.

Committee :

MORGAN THOMAS, ESQ., *Chairman.*

REV. RICHARD JONES, *Vice-Chairman.*

MR. JOHN THOMAS
    ,, JAMES MORGAN } *Churchwardens.*

REV. W. HUGH PHILLIPS	MR. JOHN BRIND
DR. R. T. E. DAVIES, J.P.	,, PHILLIP EDWARDS
MR. EDWARD EDWARDS	,, A. T. TASKER
,, JOHN EVANS, B.A.	,, JOHN WATKINS
,, A. M. DANIEL	,, SAMUEL HOLLISTER
,, JAMES SPENCER	,, DAVID THOMAS
,, WILLIAM MORGAN	,, REES SANDERS
,, G. M. G. GLASIER	,, J. H. LEWIS

Treasurer :

MR. EDWARD EDWARDS, Maesygarn, Blackwood, Mon.

Hon. Sec. :

MR. G. M. G. GLASIER, Solicitor, Blackwood, Mon.

Bankers :

LLOYDS BANK, LD.

69   Restoration of Bedwellty Parish Church, 1902

Restoration of Bedwellty Parish Church, "St. Sannan's."

COMMITTEE :—

MORGAN THOMAS, Esq., *Chairman.*
Rev. RICHARD JONES, *Vice-Chairman.*

Mr. JOHN THOMAS
Mr. JAMES MORGAN ⎱ *Churchwardens.*

Dr. R. H. E. DAVIES, J.P.
Mr. EDWARD EDWARDS.
Mr. A. M. DANIEL.
Mr. JAMES SPENCER.

Mr. G. M. G. GLASIER.
Mr. REES SAUNDERS.
Mr. D. THOMAS.
Mr. JOHN BRIND.
Mr. ALEX. ROBSON.

Mr. PHILLIP EDWARDS.
Mr. SAM HOLISTER.
Mr. A. T. TASKER.
Mr. JOHN WATKINS.

Mr. EDWARD EDWARDS, *Treasurer.*   Mr. A. T. TASKER, *Hon. Secretary*

The Committee are indebted to the Rector, the Rev. R. W. Roberts, for the valuable assistance he has given them since his advent to the Parish.

LIST OF SUBSCRIPTIONS.

	£	s.	d.
The Rt. Hon. Viscount Tredegar	120	0	0
„ „ „ Lord Llangattock	50	0	0
Mrs. Mary Brewer	37	14	4
Dr. J. D. James	25	0	0
Rep. of the late E. D. Williams	20	0	0
Miss James, Tynewydd	13	13	0
Mr. W. T. and E. Alex. James	11	1	0
„ Lewis	10	10	0
Messrs. Bargoed Coal Co., Ltd.	10	0	0
Collected by Rev. A. J. Price	8	8	6
Mr. Edmund James, Coedybrain	8	0	0
„ E. R. Lewis, Abergavenny	8	0	0
„ Thos. Jones, Plas Farm	5	5	0
„ J. Holmes, Cardiff	5	5	0
Mrs. W. M. Edwards, Punch House, Tredegar	5	0	0
Miss Emily Talbot	5	0	0
Mr. J. E. Treharne, Blackwood	4	4	0
„ D. F. Pritchard, Crumlin	2	2	0
„ W. J. Harris, Argoed Farm	1	1	0
Rev. Richard Jones	1	1	0
Mr. C. W. Ellis	1	1	0
„ Morgan Thomas, Bedwellty	1	1	0
„ John Thomas, Argoed	1	1	6
„ Edward Edwards, Maesygan House	1	1	0
Miss Thomas, Llwynmadoc	1	1	0
Mr. Evan Jones, Blackwood	1	1	0
„ Thomas Thomas Bedwellty	1	1	0
„ A. T. Tasker, Argoed	1	1	0
The Rt. Hon. Lord Penrhyn	1	1	0
Miss Jones, Rock House, Blackwood	1	1	0
Mrs. James, Coedybrain	1	1	0
Rev. R. W. Roberts, Rector of Bedwellty	1	1	0
Miss Phillips, Cardiff	1	1	0
Mrs. Dr. Richards	1	1	0
Mr. W. M. Jenkins, New Tredegar	1	1	0
„ Wm. Williams, „	1	1	0
Dr. R. H. E. Davies, „	1	1	0
Mr. Harler, New Tredegar	1	1	0
Mr. and Misses George	1	11	6
Mr. C. Tillot	1	1	0
„ C. W. Whitting	1	1	0
Carried forward £373 16 10			

	£	s.	d.
Brought forward 373 16 10			
Mr. C. Forrestier-Walker	1	1	0
„ Alex. Robson, Tredegar	1	1	0
Dr. W. W. Leigh	1	1	0
Miss Davies, Church St., Tredegar	1	0	0
Mr. Edward Spencer, Ebbw Vale	1	0	0
„ John Price, New Tredegar	1	0	0
Mrs. William White, Argoed	1	0	0
Mr. Edward Jones, Bedwellty		15	0
„ R. J. Jenkins, Argoed		15	0
Mrs. Davies, Holly Bush Inn		13	0
„ Lambert, Tredegar		13	0
Mr. J. Hardy		10	6
„ W. Hardy		10	6
Mrs. Bevan, Rhoswen House		10	6
Messrs. A. Buchan & Co., Rhymney		10	6
Mr. E. Edmunds, Blackwood		10	6
„ Lewis Jones, Blackwood		10	6
„ Rees Saunders, Bedwellty		10	6
Miss Saunders, Bedwellty		10	6
Mr. Alfred Jenkins, Tredegar		10	6
„ John Lewis, „		10	6
Dr. Brown, Tredegar		10	6
Mr. J. A. Sheppard, Tredegar		10	6
„ Jeshoida Jones, Mannoel		10	6
„ John Watkins, Galyos Farm		10	6
„ Lewis Saunders		10	6
„ Phillip Lloyd, Argoed Arms		10	0
„ R. H. Spencer, Tredegar		10	0
„ C. Hart, Blackwood		10	0
Dr. Crawford, Tredegar		10	0
Lady Hills Johns		10	0
Mr. J. John, New Tredegar		10	0
„ A. Williams		10	0
„ Tom Lewis, New Tredegar		10	0
„ John Thorley		10	0
„ John Lewis, Tredegar		10	0
„ W. H. Watkins, „		10	0
„ W. Morgan, Argoed Farm		7	6
„ T. Wiseman, New Tredegar		7	6
„ H. Judd, Tredegar		5	0
„ J. Davies		5	0
„ J. Maddocks, Rhymney		5	0
„ T. J. Price		5	0
Carried forward £398 18 4			

	£	s.	d.
Brought forward 398 18 4			
Col. Lindsay, Ystrad Mynach		5	0
Messrs. E. Jenkins & Son		5	0
„ Hutchings & May		5	0
Mrs. A. M. Charles, Argoed		5	0
Mr. Edmund Williams		5	0
„ H. Braden, Tredegar		5	0
„ A. M. James		5	0
„ David Davies, Mannoel		5	0
„ D. W. Price, New Tredegar		5	0
„ J. E. Jones, „		5	0
„ A. Russell, „		5	0
„ Gus Jones, „		5	0
Mrs. J. Price, Argoed		5	0
Mr. David Jenkins, New Tredegar		4	0
Mrs. R. Thomas, Argoed		4	0
Mr. T. A. Phillips, Tredegar		2	6
„ E. T. Morgan, Mannoel		2	6
„ Henry Jones, „		2	6
„ Geo. Phillips, „		2	6
„ Albert Jones, New Inn, Bedwellty		2	6
Mrs. Phillips, New Tredegar		2	6
Mr. J. Tillot		2	6
„ M. Jones, „		2	6
Miss Tilley Williams, Bedwellty		2	6
Mrs. Dawson		2	6
Miss Evans, P.O., Argoed		2	0
Mr. Geo. Short, Mannoel		2	0
Mrs. Dance		1	6
Mr. W. J. Walters, Mannoel		1	0
„ E. T. Walters, „		1	0
„ E. Llewellyn, „		1	0
„ P. Jones, „		1	0
„ E. Powles		1	0
Mrs. Poison			6
Re-Opening Services Offertories	6	11	4
Palm Sunday Services	1	17	3
Sunday School Offertories		7	6
From Churchwardens' Fund	1	2	1
Proceeds from Sale of History Booklets	7	5	0
Refund from L. & N.W.Rly. Co. for loss of Lamp Rods	1	0	0
£472 10 6			

70 Restoration—List of subscriptions, 1902

71   Old Tramroad, Blackwood. (Penllwyn Tramroad)

72   Old Tramroad, Woodfieldside, Blackwood

73 Hollybush Colliery workmen

74 Hollybush Colliery firemen

75 Budd's Rock Colliery, Blackwood, near Church

76 Budd's Rock Colliery, Blackwood, near Church

O 1149/R

INTERNATIONAL RUGBY FOOTBALL MATCH
WALES versus IRELAND
AT CARDIFF ARMS PARK.

ASSOCIATION FOOTBALL MATCH
Cardiff City v. Exeter City
AT NINIAN PARK

Saturday, March 14th, 1936

HALF-DAY EXCURSION

TO

CARDIFF
(QUEEN STREET)

FROM	Depart	RETURN FARES (Third Class)
	a.m.	s. d.
Brynmawr	11 0	
Beaufort	11 4	
Nantybwch	11 10	2 6
Sirhowy	11 15	
Tredegar	11 20	
Bedwellty Pits	11 25	2 0
Holly Bush	11 30	
Markham Village Halt	11 35	
Argoed	11 40	1 6
Blackwood	11 45	
Cardiff (Queen Street) ... arr.	12 31 p.m.	

RETURN ARRANGEMENTS
Passengers return same day from CARDIFF (Queen Street) at 9-40 p.m.

Children under 3 years of age, free; 3 and under 14, half-fares

CONDITIONS OF ISSUE OF EXCURSION AND OTHER TICKETS AT LESS THAN ORDINARY FARES.

These Tickets are issued subject to the Notices and Conditions shown in the Company's current Time Tables. For Luggage Allowances also see Time Tables.

All information regarding Excursion Trains on the L.M.S. Railway may be obtained at the Station, or on application to Mr. C. H. TAIT, District Goods and Passenger Manager, Victoria Station, Swansea.

March, 1936.
(E.R.O. 53302)

ASHTON DAVIES,
Chief Commercial Manager.

77   Railway Bill. Half-day Excursion to Cardiff

78 Half-day Excursion to Cardiff passing Gelli Signal Box on 14 March 1936

79 Markham Colliery Band

Courtesy of W. R. Hamer

80 Hollybush Rugby Club, 1945-46   *Courtesy of W. R. Hamer*

81 Hollybush Rugby Club, 1949-50   *Courtesy of W. R. Hamer*

82   Evans James *left* (1809-93), who wrote the words of 'Hen Wlad Fy Nhadau' and James James, son *right* (1833-1902), composer of the melody

83   Croes-Penmaen Farm. Sepia Drawing—W. W. Tasker

84 Cast-iron gates at Maesruddud Lodge

Courtesy of Cyril Jones, Argoed

Argoed Arms Hotel Quoit Ground
Argoed, Nr. Blackwood, Mon.

International Quoit Match

ENGLAND v. WALES

BANK HOLIDAY MONDAY, Aug. 6th, 1951

To commence at 2 p.m. sharp

ADMISSION, by Ticket only, 1/6 (incl. Tax)

85/86/87/88   International Quoits at Argoed

THE   ARGOED   QUOITS   CLUB

desire the pleasure of your company at a

Celebration High Tea

at the Welfare Hall, Argoed, at 7 p.m.

on

Monday, August 3rd, 1953

following the

ENGLAND v WALES International Game

W. H. Williams and C. Coles
(Joint Secretaries)

ARGOED CALLING

Cordial Greetings to everyone during this Festival year of Britain and especially to our English friends upon their first visit to Argoed.

We trust that your visit for the Thirty-Third International between the two countries will be a happy one, and hope that the Events of today will provide many pleasant memories.

To the Public the game of Quoits calls for great skill and judgment, and it is hoped that all players taking part in today's game will live up to their reputations in the grand old game.

Argoed Quoit Club has been in existence for 80 years and has been League Champions several times, the first being in 1910.

The following players have won honours while connected with Argoed: E. Morgan (later with Cwm), J. Price, B. Burston, T. Robinson, A. Withey, W. Hughes. Jack Price has the honour of winning the double, that is the Welsh Championship and Monmouthshire on three occasions.

Also at Argoed in 1933, Scotland suffered their only defeat against Wales.

We also have the honour of providing four Argoed boys for today's game, namely: T. Jenkins, J. Banks (England), and Jack Price, Ted Robinson (Wales).

1951

WELSH QUOITING ASSOCIATION

∴ CORONATION YEAR

ENGLAND v WALES

35th International on

BANK HOLIDAY MONDAY, AUGUST 3rd 1953 at

ARGOED ARMS HOTEL QUOIT GROUND
ARGOED, MON.

TEN GAMES OF 21 POINTS UP WILL BE PLAYED

Under the distinguished patronage of
Andrew Buchann's Ltd, Argoed Reform Club and S. Lloydd Esq.

**The Official Opening of the Games will take place
at 2 p.m. prompt, by Councillor W. Alderman
Chairman of Bedwellty Urban District Council.**

Referee   J. HOOK Esq., Argoed.
Official Scorers   Messrs. C. DODD and C. HILL

Groundsmen
Messrs. T. BISHOP, T. PHILLIPS, W. MORGAN T. MORGAN

Welsh Quoiting Board Officials

President :   R. PRICE Esq., Rhymney
Chairman :   L. BAKER Esq., Waunlwyd
Vice-Chairman   A. NASH Esq., Kendon

Executive :   W. Davies (Ystrad), M. James (Cwmaman), B. Wheeler (Cwmaman), I. Lewis (Merthyr), W. Donovan (Merthyr Vale).

Secretary :   A. BAKER, 22 Woodville Road, Cwm, Ebbw Vale,

SOUVENIR PROGRAMME 6d.

BLACKWOOD.

Lot 8. The Valuable and Commodious

Leasehold Shop, Dwelling Houses & Accommodation Land,

being Nos. 34 and 35 HIGH STREET, BLACKWOOD, in the occupation, as to No. 34, of Mr. George Nethercott, at the rental amounting to £8 2s. 0d., and containing Parlour, Kitchen, Pantry, Three Bedrooms, &c. ; and as to No. 35, in the occupation of Mr. E. C. Jones, at the rental of £45 per annum, payable quarterly, containing Two Sitting Rooms, Kitchen, Pantry, Scullery, &c., extensive Warehouses, Cellarage, Store Rooms and Six Bedrooms, Shop, &c., Bakehouse, Stable, Cow Houses, Pigs' Cots, with the LAND adjoining, containing **1 acre 1 rood** or thereabouts, being Nos. 303 and part of 301 on the Tithe Survey, and having Extensive Frontage to the Main Road, together with the tenancy at will of the two small fields at the rear, held at an annual rent of £1 0s. 0d.

The Property is held on lease for a term of 99 years from 25th December, 1826, at an annual Ground-rent of £7 10s. 0d. ; a small strip of the land is sub-let for the remainder of the lease, at a rental of 10s. per annum.

ARGOED.

Lot 9. The **THREE LEASEHOLD DWELLING HOUSES,** being Nos. 19, 20 and 21 HIGH STREET, ARGOED, situate near the Railway Station, with excellent GARDENS well stocked with Fruit Trees, let to Messrs. D. Thomas, Elias Smith and J. Perkins, at rentals of 19s., 10s. and 8s. per calendar month. The Land has a frontage of 173½ feet to the Main Road, and is held on lease for 99 years from May 1st, 1841, at a Ground-rent of £4.

Lot 10. The **TWO LEASEHOLD DWELLING HOUSES,** being Nos. 32 and 33 HIGH STREET, in the occupation of Mrs. M. A. Price and Mr. Hy. Bowen, at rentals of £8 per annum, payable quarterly, and 8s. per calendar month respectively. The Houses are in a good state of repair. Held on lease for a term of 99 years from May 1st, 1839, at an annual Ground-rent of £1 5s. 0d.

Lot 11. The **THREE LEASEHOLD DWELLING HOUSES,** being Nos. 5, 6 and 7 HIGH STREET, in the occupation of Messrs. J. Jenkins, E. Hall and J. Meredith, at rentals of 8s. 6d., 10s. and 8s. 6d. per calendar month respectively. The Houses are convenient and in a good state of repair, and have frontage of 70 feet to the Main Road. Held on lease for 92 years from May 1st, 1817, at an annual Ground-rent of £1 1s. 0d.

89 Houses at Blackwood & Argoed. Extract from Auction Particulars dated 30th October, 1900

90   Blackwood Station, taken after 1912 when the platforms were extended. Standing *left* is Walter Hill, the Booking Clerk, with the Station Master, H. W. Forrester *right* in a "frock coat"

Courtesy of C. H. Forrester

91   Oakdale Colliery during sinking

HOLLY BUSH COLLIERY.

No. 74   *Week ending*   **1 5 MAY 1915** *191*

Name D⁰ Davies

H.P. 42320.

	@	£	s	d	£	s	d
38. 1 3							
Brush Coal	1.9	3	6	8			
Yds Carting	8		4				
Heading							
Airways							
Days	5/-		5				
"							
Cogs	1/-		1				
Props	6d.						
Hard Coal	2d.		6	6			
Allowance							
WAR BONUS 17/8 07			1	6	8		
3/5/15							
Turning Stalls	4/9						
Working Double							
" Nights	3d.						
Minimum Make Up							
Compensation ......Wks......Dys							
Advance 60 %		2 9 9	7	19	5		
Less Draw							
" Insurance			4				
" Doctor		1	4				
" Rent							
" House Coal T C							
" Haulage			3				
" Subscription to Library							
" War Fund							
" Helves							
" Wood							
" Train Fare			6				
" Check Weigher			3				
" Explosives						4	8
Balance Due					7	14	9

92 Payment of Wages. D. Davies, Hollybush Colliery, 1915

109

LONDON HOUSE,

SUNNY VIEW, ARGOED, Mon.

Oct 22nd 1918

Mr Tasker

Bot. of ISAIAH JENKINS

Draper and Outfitter.

93 Billhead for Isaiah Jenkins, Argoed. Property burnt to the ground in early 1920's

94 Billhead from Brinley Jenkins, Argoed, 1927

115

192

Mrs Tasker

Bought of **B. JENKINS,**

Baker, Grocer and Provision Merchant,

34, High Street, ARGOED, Mon.

WEIGHT TICKET OR CONSIGNMENT NOTE
On Delivery of Coal, over Two Hundredweight, in bulk, by Cart.

CHRISTOPHER POND, COLLIERY PROPRIETOR, Blackwood, Mon.

........................191...

Mr................................   TONS CWT. QRS.

Take Notice that you are to receive
herewith of Coal

                      T.   C.   Q.

Weight of Coal and Vehicl
Tare Weight of Vehicle......
   Nett Weight of Coal herewith
   delivered to Purchaser............

                             For C. POND.

   Driver in Charge of Cart.

Received by................................
   Where Coal is delivered by means of a Vehicle, the Seller must deliver or send by
Post or otherwise to the Purchaser or his Servant, before any part of the Coal is
unloaded, a Ticket or Note in this Form.
   Any Seller who delivers a less quantity than is stated in this Ticket or Note is
liable to a fine.
   Any Person attending on a Vehicle used for the delivery of Coals who, having
received a Ticket or Note for delivery to the Purchaser, refuses or neglects to deliver
it to the Purchaser or his Servant is liable to a Fine.

95   Consignment Note for delivery of Coal, 1923—
Christopher Pond, Blackwood, 1918

96   Consignment Note for delivery of Coal, 1923—
Rhoswen Colliery, Argoed, 1918

Rhoswen Colliery, Argoed,

.................191

M Tasker

Bot. of LEWIS PRICE.

7701

Weight Ticket or Consignment Note
On Delivery of Coal, over Two Hundredweight, in bulk, by Cart.

BOWDITCH BROS. LTD. COLLIERY PROPRIETORS, Blackwood, Mon.

23/10/23 192

Mr. *Tasker*	TONS	CWT.	QR
Take Notice that you are to receive herewith of Coal Two	1	0	0
	T.	C.	Q.

Weight of Coal and Vehicle

Tare Weight of Vehicle

Net Weight of Coal herewith delivered to Purchaser

S. John   **For BOWDITCH BROS. LTD.**

Driver in Charge of Cart.

Received by

Where Coal is delivered by means of a Vehicle, the Seller must deliver or send by Post or otherwise to the Purchaser or his Servant, before any part of the Coal is unloaded, a Ticket or Note in this Form.

Any Seller who delivers a less quantity than is stated in this Ticket or Note is liable to a fine.

Any Person attending on a Vehicle used for the delivery of Coals who, having received a Ticket or Note for delivery to the Purchaser, refuses or neglects to deliver it to the Purchaser or his Servant is liable to a fine.

S. Bros. Ltd. 36530

97   Consignment Note for delivery of Coal, 1923—
Bowditch Bros. Ltd., Blackwood, 1923

98   Consignment Note for delivery of Coal, 1923—
Rock Colliery, Blackwood

110

ROCK COLLIERY, BLACKWOOD, Mon.

WEIGHT TICKET, OR CONSIGNMENT NOTE,
On Delivery of Coal, over Two Hundredweight, in bulk, by Cart.

3/1/1923 .... 192 3

Mr. *Tasker*	Tons	Cwt.	Qrs.
Take Notice that you are to receive herewith of Coal	1	0	0
	T.	C.	Q.

Weight of Coal and Vehicle

Tare Weight of Vehicle 12/6

Nett Weight of Coal herewith delivered to Purchaser *Paid 14-0*

     For BUDD & COMPANY, Ltd.

M Williams

Driver in Charge of Cart.

Where Coal is delivered by means of a Vehicle, the Seller must deliver or send by Post or otherwise to the Purchaser or his Servant, before any part of the Coal is unloaded, a Ticket or Note in this form.

Any Seller who delivers a less quantity than is stated in this Ticket or Note is liable to a Fine.

Any person attending on a Vehicle used for the Delivery of Coals who, having received a Ticket or Note for delivery to the Purchaser, refuses or neglects to deliver it to the Purchaser or his Servant is liable to a Fine.

Form authorised by the County Council; sold by Hughes & Son, Pontypool.

Bedwellty School Board Election

MONDAY NEXT, May 20th, 1901.

LIST OF CANDIDATES.

No.	SURNAME.	OTHER NAMES.
1	BARRETT	ALFRED
2	DAVID	DAVID PHILLIP
3	DAVIES	THOMAS LLOYD
4	DENT	FREDERICK
5	EVANS	HOWELL THOMAS
6	EVANS	JOHN ARTHUR
7	FISHER	DANIEL
8	ONIONS	ALFRED
9	PHILLIPS	BENJAMIN
10	PRICE	DAVID WILLIAM
11	PRICE	JOHN WILLIAM
12	REES	DAVID MORGAN
13	REES	JOHN ALFRED
14	RICHARDS	THOMAS
15	TALLIS	ALFRED SIMEON
16	THOMAS	JOHN DANIEL
17	THOMAS (Ap Noah)	JOHN
18	THOMAS	JOHN
19	WATKINS	LEWIS
20	WILLPUTTE	NESTOR LOUIS

Plump for HOWELL THOMAS EVANS

(Dr. Evans), No. 5 on the Ballot Paper.

The Poll will be open from 8 a.m. till 8 p.m.

Printed and Published by A. M'Lay & Co., 9, Duke St., Cardiff

The Laurels,
Blackwood.
May 13th, 1901.

Hoping to be favored with
your vote and interest

Yours faithfully
Howell Thomas Evans

99 Dr. Howell Thomas Evans, The Laurels, Blackwood. Local Election, 1901

100 Bedwellty Parish Church. Drawing by W. W. Tasker

101 Libanus School about 1915

102 Sirhowy Railway Locomotive used between Sirhowy and Newport from 1860 to 1876

103 Hollybush Colliery Wagon.   *E. D. Williams*

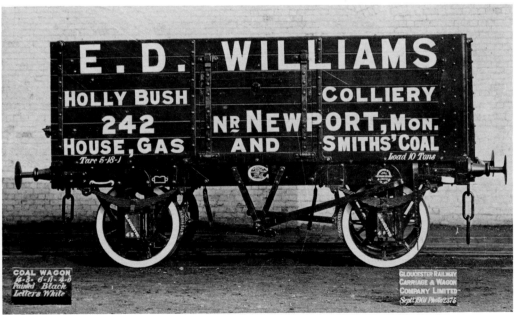

104 William Lewis Meredith. Founder Permanent Way
Institution

The above named was the last of the Meredith family to work on the
maintenance of the Permanent Way of the Sirhowy Line. He was born
in 1843 and died in 1924. His father, William Meredith, born in 1809,
died in 1886. The third member of the family was William Lewis ap
Meredydd, who was born in 1760, and died in 1836. He was responsible
for much of the original Tramway construction from Sirhowy to Nine
Mile Point. Both William Lewis Meredith and his father were born in
Argoed. The paternal ancestors were descended from Llewelyn, the
third son of Gwilym ap Philip of Rhiwbina, by Cardiff, who settled at
Gwrhay, in the Parish of Mynyddislwyn, *c.*1425

105 Budd's Rock Colliery, Blackwood. *Colin Spencer*

106 Argoed School Staff, 1919. Rear—Evan Williams, Olwen Phillips (Mrs. Hemming), Miss Arnott, Eddie Jones. Front—Miss Herrington, Mr. Hough (Headmaster), Gladys Panes

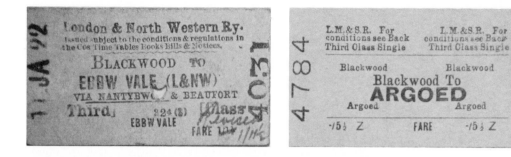

107 Railway Tickets issued by local stations   *Courtesy of Malcolm James*

O 1461/R

RUGBY LEAGUE INTERNATIONAL MATCH
WALES v. ENGLAND
At TAFF VALE PARK, PONTYPRIDD
Kick-off 3-0 p.m.—SATURDAY, NOVEMBER 7th

Saturday, November 7th, 1936

HALF-DAY EXCURSION to

PONTYPRIDD

FROM	DEPART	RETURN FARES (Third Class)
	p.m.	s. d.
BRYNMAWR	12 40	
EBBW VALE	12 35	2 6
BEAUFORT	12 50	
NANTYBWCH	1 0	
SIRHOWY	1 10	2 0
TREDEGAR	1 15	
*BEDWELLTY PITS	1 20	
HOLLY BUSH	1 25	1 6
MARKHAM V. HALT	1 30	
ARGOED	1 35	
BLACKWOOD	1 40	1 3
PONTYPRIDD ... ... arr.	2 31 p.m.	

RETURN ARRANGEMENTS
Passengers return from Pontypridd at 7-5 p.m. same day.
*—Tickets must be obtained in advance from Tredegar or Holly Bush.

Children under 3 years of age, free; 3 and under 14, half-fares.

CONDITIONS OF ISSUE OF EXCURSION AND OTHER TICKETS AT LESS THAN ORDINARY FARES.

These Tickets are issued subject to the Notices and Conditions shown in the Company's current Time Tables. For Luggage Allowances also see Time Tables.

Further particulars and tickets in advance may be obtained at the Stations and Agencies.

All information regarding cheap travel and other facilities on the London Midland and Scottish Railway will be supplied on application to the Stations, Agencies, or Mr. C. H. TAIT, District Goods and Passenger Manager, Victoria Station, SWANSEA (Telephone 2161, Ex. 14).

October, 1936.
(E.R.O. 53302)

ASHTON DAVIES,
Chief Commercial Manager.

(4000)   Swale Service, Widnes.—14596   O 1461/R

108   Railway Billhead. Half-day Excursion to Pontypridd. November 1936

109　Mrs. Harriet Bevan, wife of Walter Bevan.
Mr. Bevan was a noted surveyor and a partner in
the Rhoswen Colliery Co. of Bevan & Pryce in
the 1870's. Mrs. Bevan (daughter of Thomas
Ellis, Engineer, Tredegar) kept the Rhoswen
Shop at the Rock.　*Courtesy of Mrs. Olwen Hemming*

110　Blackwood. View looking towards Argoed. Royal Oak Inn on right, where Inquests were
held on those killed or injured underground or on the Tramroad

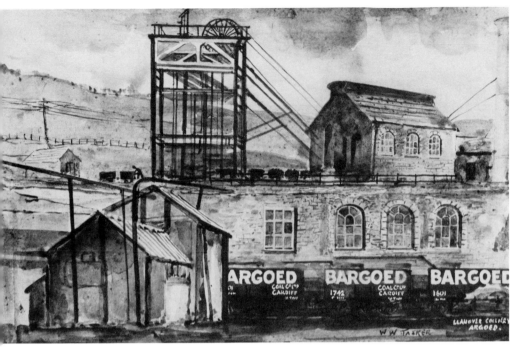

111 Llanover Colliery, Argoed. Sepia drawing, 1928. W. W. Tasker

112 Bedwellty Church Bells. Photographed in 1988 during restoration of Tower and Bells

Courtesy of Gerald Davies

O 1115/R

INTERNATIONAL RUGBY FOOTBALL MATCH

WALES versus NEW ZEALAND

AT CARDIFF ARMS PARK.   KICK-OFF 2-30 p.m.

Saturday, December 21st, 1935

HALF-DAY EXCURSION

TO

CARDIFF

(QUEEN STREET)

FROM	Depart	RETURN FARES (Third Class)	
	a.m.	s.	d.
Brynmawr	11 0		
Beaufort	11 4		
Nantybwch	11 10	2	6
Sirhowy	11 15		
Tredegar	11 20		
Bedwellty Pits	11 25	2	0
Holly Bush	11 30		
Markham Village Halt	11 35		
Argoed	11 40	1	6
Blackwood	11 45		
Cardiff (Queen Street) ... arr.	12 31 p.m.		

RETURN ARRANGEMENTS

Passengers return same day from CARDIFF (Queen Street) at 9-40 p.m.

Children under 3 years of age, free; 3 and under 14, half-fares.

CONDITIONS OF ISSUE OF EXCURSION AND OTHER TICKETS AT LESS THAN ORDINARY FARES.

These Tickets are issued subject to the Notices and Conditions shown in the Company's current Time Tables. For Luggage Allowances also see Time Tables.

All information regarding Excursion Trains on the L.M.S. Railway may be obtained at the Station, or on application to Mr. C. H. TAIT, District Goods and Passenger Manager, Victoria Station, Swansea.

December, 1935.   **ASHTON DAVIES,**
(E.R.O. 53302)   **Chief Commercial Manager.**

113   L.M.S. Half-day Excursion to Cardiff, 1935

O1597/R

THURSDAY, JULY 8th, 1937
DAY EXCURSION to
Hereford, Gt. Malvern, Worcester
BIRMINGHAM and COVENTRY

FROM	DEPART	RETURN FARES (Third Class)				
		Hereford	Gt. Malvern	Worcester (F. St.)	Birmingham (NewSt.)	Coventry
	a.m.	s. d.	s. d.	s. d.	s. d.	s. d.
Merthyr	6 50	5 0	7 0	7 6	9 0	10 6
Cefn Coed Halt ... A	6 55					
Pantysgallog Halt ... B	7 5	4 6	6 6	7 0	8 6	10 0
Dowlais (High Street) ...	7 10					
Rhymney Bridge	7 20	4 0	6 0			
Pontllanfraith	6 50	5 6			9 0	10 6
Blackwood	6 55		7 0	7 6		
Argoed ... ... E	7 0					
Markham Village Halt ... E	7 10	5 0	6 6			
Holly Bush	7 15		6 6		8 6	10 0
Bedwellty Pits ... G	7 20	4 6		7 0		
Tredegar	7 25					
Sirhowy	7 30	4 0	6 0			
Nantybwch	7 35					
Ebbw Vale	7 20			6 6		
Beaufort	7 45					
Brynmawr	8 0	3 6	5 6		8 0	9 6
Gelli Felen Halt ... C	8 10			6 0		
Clydach Halt ... ... D	8 15					
Gilwern Halt ... ... D	8 20	3 0	5 0	5 6		
Govilon	8 25					
Abergavenny (Brecon Rd.) ...	8 35	2 6	4 6		7 6	9 0
Abergavenny Jct.	8 45					
Arrivals		9-24 a.m.	10-5 a.m.	10-20a.m.	11-28 a.m.	12-6 p.m.

Tickets to be obtained in advance :—
- A—at Merthyr
- B— ,, Dowlais
- C— ,, Brynmawr
- D—at Govilon
- E— ,, Argoed or Markham V Halt.
- G— ,, Holly Bush or Tredegar

RETURN ARRANGEMENTS
Passengers return same day leaving Coventry 9-28 p.m., Birmingham (New St.) 10-35 p.m., Worcester (F. St.) 11-25 p.m., Great Malvern 11-42 p.m., and Hereford 12-50, 3-35, 4-15, 6-20, 8-20 p.m. or 12-22 a.m. (night).

*—Passengers for Coventry change at Birmingham in each direction.

Children under 3 years of age, free; 3 and under 14, half-fares.

CONDITIONS OF ISSUE OF EXCURSION AND OTHER TICKETS AT LESS THAN ORDINARY FARES

These Tickets are issued subject to the Notices and Conditions shown in the Company's current Time Tables. For Luggage Allowances also see Time Tables.

All information regarding cheap travel and other facilities on the London Midland and Scottish Railway will be supplied on application to Mr. C. H. TAIT, District Goods and Passenger Manager, Victoria Station, SWANSEA (Telephone 2161, Extension 14).

May, 1937.
(E.R.O. 53302)

ASHTON DAVIES,
Chief Commercial Manager.

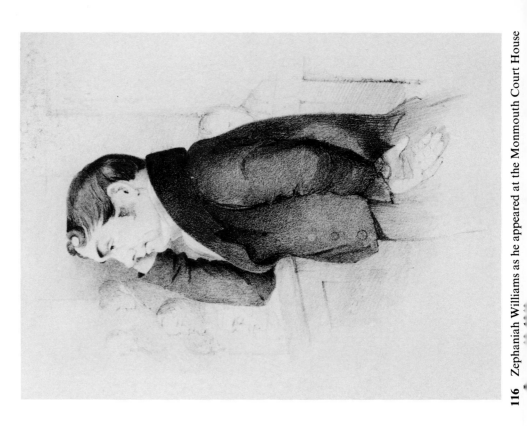

116 Zephaniah Williams as he appeared at the Monmouth Court House

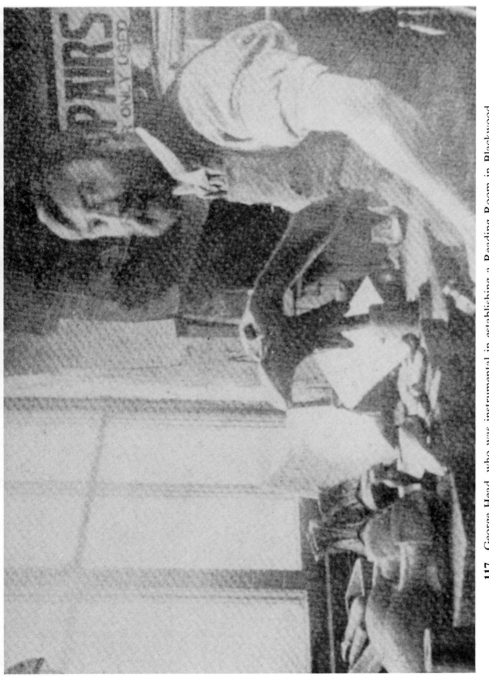

117 George Head, who was instrumental in establishing a Reading Room in Blackwood.
'Argus' Reporter and Shoe Maker, he walked with aid of crutches

118   'Perseverance'—2nd Wesleyan Chapel, Blackwood

119   3rd Wesleyan Chapel, Blackwood

120 Mount Pleasant Baptist Chapel, Blackwood

121 Mount Pleasant Baptist Sunday School. Teachers and Officers, Past and Present. 1925

122 'Joe, the Doctor' and car. Chauffeur and Handyman for Dr. Howell Evans, Blackwood
(see caption 99)

Courtesy of James Lewis

123 Pont-Abernant-y-Felin, carrying the Bedwellty to Manmoel road.
Pencil Drawing, W. W. Tasker

124 Pont-Syr-Dafydd at the Rock. Sepia, W. W. Tasker. Mentioned by Archdeacon Coxe in his book 'An Historical Tour of Monmouthshire' published 1801

125   Black Rock, near Pont-Abernant-y-felin. Winter 1921

126   Blackwood Station and Carpenters Arms from the road, looking towards Tredegar

127 Budd's Rock Colliery,
Blackwood

128 Mr. Cyril Davies, of Markham is the proud possessor of a watch which was presented to
his grandfather, James Davies in 1912, and inscribed as follows:— 'Presented to James Davies
by the Directors of the Markham Steam Coal Co. for heroism at the Markham Explosion,
18 May, 1912'   *Courtesy of Gerald Davies*

Easter Day, 1918.

"The third day, He rose again from the dead."

Parish Church.

Holy Communion at 7 and 11 a.m.

S. Peter's, Aberbargoed.

Holy Communion at 7.30, 9 and 11 a.m.

Holly Bush.

Holy Communion at 9 a.m.

"Christ our Passover is sacrificed for us, therefore let us keep the Feast."—*1 Cor. v. 7, 8.*

...nclose an envelope for your Easter Offering, which will be given, as usual, to the A.C.S.

R. W. ROBERTS,

Rector.

Our Easter Wish.

May the Risen Christ, Who left His Home for us, have you in His keeping till we meet again.

PARISH OF BEDWELLTY. *Four Words No. 160*

Courtesy of James Lewis

129 Bedwellty Easter Card (2 sides)

130 Llanover Colliery

131 Original Maesruddud Farm before rebuilding in 1890 *Courtesy of James Lewis*

132 Early photograph of the 'Williams' family, Maesruddud   *Courtesy of James Lewis*

133 The Coleman brothers

134 Miss Margaret Williams, Maesruddud on the occasion of presentation at Court

Courtesy of James Lewis

135 Christopher Pond (in chair) and Sam Phillips (bowling). Others believed to be Messrs Love and Gittins

Courtesy of Mrs. Olwen Hemming

136 The Westgate Hotel was founded in 1709, Samuel Dean, Proprietor; and was entirely rebuilt on a magnificent scale in 1887 from the designs of A. E. Landsdowne, Architect. The interior was carried out in the style of the Italian Renaissance, but the original pillars of the vestibule, showing Chartists bullet marks were retained when rebuilding

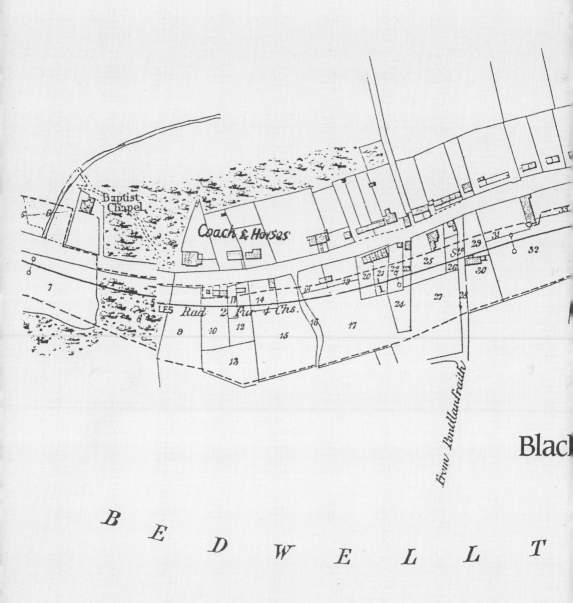

Baptist Chapel

Coach & Horses

LE5 Rud 2 Fur 4 Chs.

6

2

7

5

8

9

11

14

10

12

15

13

16

18

19

17

20

21

23

24

27

25

26

28

29

30

31

32

St

Ffrw Pontllanfraith

Blac

B   E   D   W   E   L   L   T